Communicating with Quotes
THE IGBO CASE

JOYCE PENFIELD

Contributions in Intercultural and Comparative Studies, Number 8

GREENWOOD PRESS
Westport, Connecticut • London, England

Library of Congress Cataloging in Publication Data

Penfield, Joyce.
  Communicating with quotes.

  (Contributions in intercultural and comparative studies, ISSN 0147-1031; no. 8)
  Bibliography: p.
  Includes index.
  1. Proverbs, Igbo—Social aspects. 2. Igbo (African people)—Social life and customs. 3. Quotation.
4. Interpersonal conflict. I. Title. II. Series.
PN6519.I33P46   1983   398'.9'96332   82-15626
ISBN 0-313-23767-0 (lib. bdg.)

Copyright © 1983 by Joyce Penfield

All rights reserved. No portion of this book may be reproduced, by any process or technique, without the express written consent of the publisher.

Library of Congress Catalog Card Number: 82-15626
ISBN: 0-313-23767-0
ISSN: 0147-1031

First published in 1983

Greenwood Press
A division of Congressional Information Service, Inc.
88 Post Road West, Westport, Connecticut 06881

Printed in the United States of America

10 9 8 7 6 5 4 3 2 1

To my children
Anyiam, Amaechi, and Adanna Okezie

CONTENTS

	Illustrations	ix
	Tables	xi
	Preface	xiii
CHAPTER 1	DEFINING QUOTING BEHAVIOR	1
	Scope of Study	1
	The Nature of Quoting Behavior	3
	Functional Properties	4
	Notes	13
CHAPTER 2	STUDYING QUOTING BEHAVIOR	17
	Theory of the Use of Proverbs	17
	Fundamental Assumptions	20
	Field Methods	24
	Sample	25
	Analysis	28
	Notes	29
CHAPTER 3	ETHNOGRAPHY OF QUOTING BEHAVIOR	31
	Introduction	31
	The Setting	31
	Network of Social Relationships	35
	Interpersonal Relationships: Friend and Enemy	43
	Folk Conceptions	44
	Semiotics of Conflict	47

	Management of Conflict	48
	Communicative Stages of Conflict	50
	Conflict Sequence	54
	Interactional Roles and Communicative Strategies	62
	Skill in Communicating	68
	Notes	72
CHAPTER 4	IGBO THEMES	76
	Definition of "Theme"	76
	Notes	83
CHAPTER 5	COMMUNICATING IN QUOTES AROUND THE WORLD	85
	Quoting Behavior Among Bilinguals	85
	Universality	87
	Future Research	90
APPENDIX A	Glossary of Igbo Terms	93
APPENDIX B	Selected Passages from Mukařovský (1971)	96
APPENDIX C	Flow Chart of Conflict Sequence	105
APPENDIX D	Reference List of Proverbs	111
	Bibliography	121
	General Subject Index	133

ILLUSTRATIONS

1. Map of Igbo-speaking Area   27
2. Hierarchy of Social Units among the Owerri Igbo   34
3. Conflict Cycle   60
4. Relationship between Skill, Status Position, and Role   71

TABLES

I.	Follow-up Questions Used for Ethnographic Interviewing	25
II.	Mediators	38
III.	Offenses Leading to Conflict	49
IV.	Proverbs Quoted in Interactional Events	50
V.	Obvious Stages in Conflict Development	51

PREFACE

This research is an outgrowth not only of a scholarly interest in what the use of language reflects about culture but also of a personal interest and commitment to the members of Igbo society. According to one Igbo proverb: *Mmùo kpàrà nwatà ò gbàgbùǫ ele, gà ènyere ya aka ò màvụrụ ya.* (L.T. [Literal Translation] The spirit who helps a child to shoot an antelope will also help him to carry it home.) Thus my curiosity and interest in understanding more than the superficial aspects of Igbo culture and more than how Western societies view Igbo society has motivated a great deal of this study.

In addition, my interest was increased as a result of close contact with different members of Igbo society over a period of ten years, both in the United States and in Nigeria. In part, this study served to satisfy my own curiosity for a deeper insight into how members of the Igbo ethnic group view the world.

I am grateful for the assistance of Paul L. Garvin, Professor of Linguistics, State University of New York-Buffalo, and Madeleine Mathiot, Professor of Linguistics, State University of New York-Buffalo. Their scholarly suggestions as well as their personal interest are greatly appreciated.

May members of the Igbo ethnic group who have contributed to this study by serving as respondents, especially those residing in Buffalo, New York; students and staff members at Alvan Ikoku College of Education, Owerri, Nigeria; members of the village-group of Uturu in Okigwe Division; and my ex-husband, James Okezie, who is well-versed in traditional Igbo society. Especially helpful to me were my former in-laws, members of the village of Aro, Uturu. Their kindness to me during all of my visits to Nigeria over a period of ten years is much appreciated. I am also grateful to the Marist brothers of Uturu, who unselfishly provided me with necessary accommodations and support while I conducted my field work in that area, and a colleague, Bertram Osuagwu, who checked my Igbo orthography and tone marking.

Communicating with Quotes

CHAPTER 1
DEFINING QUOTING BEHAVIOR

Ejì ụkà ème ụka.[1]

L.T. Use speech in making a speech.[2]
P.T. Quote past events for present circumstances.[3]

SCOPE OF STUDY

This book reports on the analytical findings of a study of a particular type of verbal behavior in an African society--the Igbo society in southeastern Nigeria.[4] The type of verbal behavior discussed in this book will be referred to as <u>quoting behavior</u>, that is, the use of quotes to communicate a message.[5] Quoting behavior plays an extremely important role in the daily life of Igbo society. Traditionally this type of verbal behavior is manifested through Igbo proverbs. As a result of the introduction of Christianity and the English language to the Igbo society, it is also manifested in the use of Biblical sayings, English proverbs, and quotes from classical English literature, particularly Shakespeare. The study on which this book is based was primarily interested in understanding more about the nature of quoting behavior and its function in Igbo society. However, the examples of quoting behavior offered in this work focus only on the use of Igbo proverbs in conflict situations.

Proverbs are a highly prevalent and prestigious form of speech in Igbo society as well as most other African societies (Finnegan, 1970: 389). They serve to illustrate a basic principle noted by Hymes (1964: 39), a sociolinguist and a pioneer in the "ethnography of communication." ". . . language [and its different genres] is [are] not everywhere equivalent in role and value."6 This principle has not been fully pursued in regard to the use of proverbs in different cultural communities. Despite the importance of proverbs and quoting behavior in general in a multitude of African societies, there have been hardly any satisfactory investigations dealing with why, how, and by or among whom proverbs are used (Finnegan, 1970: 394) or with the range of social uses and typical interactional settings in which proverbs are used in any one society (Abrahams, 1972: 119). In addition to this, where there is a thorough description of interactional settings given, rarely is there any in-depth analysis which attempts to explain what effects proverbs are intended to achieve for the interlocutors or audience that <u>ordinary</u> language would not achieve and why this is so (Herskovits, 1930).7 In short, there has been an overemphasis on recording proverb texts <u>without</u> also treating interactional settings (Arewa, 1970: 430). Therefore, there is clearly a need for a detailed analysis of the use of proverbs in their interactional settings. It is conceived by this researcher that a study of quoting behavior or the use of proverbs in a specific society can not only reveal significant patterns and values of that particular society but also can suggest concepts useful in constructing a theory of quoting behavior or a theory of the use of proverbs. These are two additional broad goals of the analysis of this research.

The methodological approach utilized in this study derives from a key observation made by Mukařovský, a literary member of the Prague school, as well as members of different African societies where proverbs are frequently used: the proverb is tied to its interactional setting (colloquially termed <u>situation</u> or <u>context</u>).8 As a member of Fante culture noted to a fieldworker: "There is no proverb without the situation." (Christensen, 1958: 233). An Igbo proverb points out what the Fante speaker meant: *Ihe ilu̟ mee, à tu̟a ilu.* (L.T. When a situation that needs a proverb occurs, then a proverb is created). Thus, given the crucial importance of the interactional setting to the use of proverbs, this research deals in detail with interactional settings in which proverbs are used. The approach used in this work then consists of collecting a variety of different proverbs in one or more different interactional settings typical of Owerri Igbo society and then analyzing similar interactional settings for those factors which can explain why the proverb is quoted and the effect(s) it is intended to have.

The approach to this research was empirical and ethnographic. The data on which this book is based consists mainly of about 100 narrative descriptions and interpretations of interactional settings in which proverbs could appropriately be quoted which were elicited in English from thirty-five male and female Igbo-English bilinguals from Imo State, Nigeria. These respondents offered "folk verbal accounts" in the form of recollections of actual interactional events and hypothetical interactional events in which specific proverbs could be quoted.9 These recollections along with interpretations served as the data of analysis.

There are at least two advantages to the reliance on folk conceptions in this investigation of the use of proverbs. First, interactional settings which serve as the unit of analysis for the investigation of the use of proverbs are defined by the members of the culture rather than the researcher or analyst. That is, both specific types of interactional settings and the boundaries of any one interactional setting are determined by the <u>folk</u> or members of Owerri Igbo culture themselves. Secondly, by relying on folk conceptions for the collection of most of the interactional settings, this research could avoid an ethnocentric approach to the study of quoting behavior in Owerri Igbo society and thus provide "a way of seeing the culture inside-out instead of outside-in" (Dundes, 1967: 128).

The analysis sought answers to three broad but inter-related questions: (1) Why is quoting behavior used rather than other types of "ordinary" verbal behavior in Igbo society? (2) What are the properties of quotes that allow them to function as they do in quoting behavior? and (3) What are the "immediate" and "ultimate" functions of quoting behavior in Igbo society?[10]

Finally, this book extends beyond an ethnographic description of quoting behavior in one particular society. The analytical findings suggest implications for many other societies of the world, both African and non-African and also raise questions about universals and the nature of quoting behavior.

THE NATURE OF QUOTING BEHAVIOR

Viewing the uses of proverbs as the manifestation of a particular type of verbal behavior places proverbs in a broader frame-of-reference than they have traditionally been placed in any previous research. This distinction is owed to Mukařovský, a literary member of the Prague school, who notes that proverbs are often used as quotes "to indicate something the speaker for whatever reason does not wish to say directly" (Mukařovský, 1971). The study of Igbo society drawn on in this book also provides empirical justification for placing proverbs in the broader category of quoting behavior.

A very convincing empirical justification for treating proverbs as a manifestation of quoting behavior is the Igbo folk conception of proverbs as quotes. This folk view was clearly reflected in an interview with one Igbo speaking respondent who offered the following comment about proverbs: "The proverb gives credence to what you are saying; it is quoting the experts." With no prior mention by the researcher of proverbs as quotes, this respondent repeatedly made reference to "quoting." Such a folk conception is easy to understand when one looks at a proverb in the process of being born in Igbo society. Often, the creator or originator is mentioned by the community who knows him, for example, "As Chief_____ says, . . .", but as time passes or as the proverb is used by different communities the name of the originator is dropped, leaving only the proverb. This process by which many proverbs originate serves as another empirical justification for treating proverbs as quotes.

Empirical observations of bilingual Igbo-English memebers of Igbo society also offer justification for treating proverbs as one way in which quoting behavior is manifested. Nowadays quotes in English are used as documentation to perform the same functions in highly literate Igbo communities as proverbs do in traditional Igbo communities. In Christian communities Biblical statements are commonly quoted as documentation while in communities which aspire to education and Western ways, English proverbs and literary works, especially those from Shakespeare, are more commonly quoted. Thus, since quoting behavior in Igbo society utilizes a variety of different types of quotes to fulfill the same function in the lives of the users, there is empirical justification for treating the use of proverbs as a type of quoting behavior.

A final justification for treating the use of proverbs as a type of quoting behavior is based on data from other cultures. In a study of a white, suburban, Christian community in Georgia, Greenhouse (1976) notes the use of Biblical quotes among members of the religious group to resolve and control conflicts. The interesting thing about Greenhouse's study is that Biblical quotes in this American society are apparently used in almost exactly the same way as proverbs are used in Igbo society: to prevent open expression of conflicts by allowing the addressee a chance to react to an abstract and less threatening situation. Accounts rendered from ethnographers (Finnegan, 1970) about other African societies allude to the use of proverbs to fulfill this same function. This cross-cultural data suggests that perhaps quoting behavior has some universal properties which are manifested differentially depending upon social values of the community of users. Some properties of quoting behavior suggested by this research on Igbo society will now be discussed. Whether or not they are universal to quoting behavior throughout the world remains to be determined through more comparative data.

The work reported in this book is based on a functionalist empiricist view of language behavior.[11] Therefore, the study was based on the working assumption that quoting behavior as manifested in the use of proverbs plays an important role in the lives of those who quote and that this role, which serves to define function, can be uncovered through careful analysis of this behavior. The function of quoting behavior in Igbo society will be discussed after the presentation of data.

FUNCTIONAL PROPERTIES

Quoting behavior is a useful alternative to "ordinary" speech or non-quoting behavior.[12] Not everyone in Igbo society is equally skilled in quoting behavior although most aspire to be so because a skillful use of quotes can often help the speakers achieve their communicative goals more readily than can the use of other types of verbal behavior. This research on Igbo society suggests five defining properties of quotes which account for their effectiveness. These will be referred to here as "functional properties" since they are defined in terms of their social function rather than their linguistic structure. Some of the potentially universal properties can be explained by the linguistic characteristics of the quote while others can only be explained by the societal values and attitudes toward verbal behavior in general. The five functional properties will be referred to as: (1) depersonalization; (2) foregrounding; (3) authoritativeness; (4) reference to societal norms and values; and (5) prestige.

Depersonalization

Depersonalization is one of the essential qualities of the quote in that this process allows the message conveyed to be done indirectly and impersonally, since it does not belong to any particular participant of the interaction involved. Depersonalization allows the speaker to bring out a very sensitive matter in a nondefinite or abstract manner; as a result, speakers are not held personally responsible for their statements. Thus depersonalization can protect the participants from open shame and embarrassment and it always protects the speaker from implications, such as slander, and involvement in the message being conveyed. When used by a speaker as a tool of positive persuasion, depersonalization obviously serves to reduce the possibility of the speaker and addressee entering into interpersonal conflict with one another and thereby beginning a new conflict rather than settling the original one. The importance of depersonalization is illustrated by the proverb used below by a mediator to make peace between two disputants.

> Two men, Dike and Oko, were friends. They got into a quarrel one day. Hearing the quarrel, an older male, Imo, rushed in to break up the quarrel and then he tried to peacefully settle the matter. He heard the complaints from Dike and then Oko. Then, he decided that Dike had caused the quarrel. Therefore, he advised Dike that what he had done was wrong: "*Mmadù àdighì àma ṅgbè o gàfèrè n'ama ibe ogọ̀ ya.*" (L.T. You never know when you cross into your in-law's compound.) One never knows that the person he mistreats may some day be closely related to him or even in charge of supervising him.

Thus, the mediator's use of the proverb in the illustrated situation above served to point out a mistake to one disputant, to encourage the disputant to accept the blame, and to avoid implicating the mediator as being biased or unfair in his decision.

At the same time depersonalization can also be used by a speaker to launch an attack by insulting an addressee in front of others with the use of quotes. The case below illustrates this use of quotes particularly well.

> Oti, a middle-aged man, did not get along with the relative of another man, Okorie. Because Oti treated Okorie's relative badly, Okorie viewed Oti as his enemy. He sought an opportunity to revenge. One day this opportunity came

during a public meeting where many men in the community had
gathered to discuss community matters. Oti stood up and
made an impractical suggestion to the group. Recognizing
that this suggestion was not very intelligent, especially
for a man of Oti's age, Okorie took advantage of this
opportunity to insult Oti before the group. Okorie began
his own speech by saying: "*Nwatà kwùe okwù, à màrà kà
àhu ya ra.*" (L.T. When a child speaks his maturity is
portrayed.) That is, Oti had spoken and now everyone could
see how stupid he was. Thus, Okorie had demeaned Oti in
public. Oti, indeed, felt very insulted and angry.

This example illustrates the skillful way in which the depersonalized nature of a quote is used to protect the speaker from repercussions he might incur as a result of the addressee's anger at being insulted or even more significantly at being subtly defeated in public.

The depersonalization of the quote no doubt stems from the nature of quoting behavior but as far as the use of proverbs is concerned it also stems from the internal (formal) aspects of the proverb. The "frozen" word order and archaic lexicon help to mark the statement as uniquely that of someone other than the speaker.[13] Igbo proverbs have impersonal verbal forms and other linguistic devices which also add to the impersonal nature of the proverb as a quote.[14]

In his discussion on a theory of proverbs, Mukařovský (1971) attributes this depersonalization to the fact that the speaker who uses the proverb is not in fact its originator. Quoting allows what Mukařovský terms "third party intrusion," that is an outside party (speaker) speaks through the mouth of the speaker. The speaker can take a certain evaluative position to the matter at hand and encourage the listener and/or addressee to take the same position. Thus depersonalization makes the quote a powerful tool of persuasion.

Foregrounding

Foregrounding is another functional property of quotes, perhaps more typical of proverbs than other types of quotes.[15] This functional property is defined in terms of the interactional setting in which the quote is embedded. Mukařovský (1971) notes that ". . . the proverb lives . . . a complete life only in context." Even though the quote is felt to be an integral part of its interactional setting, it is also felt to be a foreign element. This notion is similar to Mukařovský's "deautomization" (Mukařovský, 1978) which he used more generally to explain the aesthetic efficacy of art. Basically, Mukařovský was referring to the hierarchy of interrelations among various elements involved in a piece of art. Applied to the use of proverbs or quotes in an interactional discourse, the proverb is both an integral part of the interactional discourse and a foreign element in it since its semantic form and internal vocabulary and/or structure usually mark it as contrasting with the surrounding literal speech.

Because of their metaphorical nature, proverbs are often ambiguous outside of a specific interactional context. Because of this "foreigness" or contrast with the surrounding discourse context, speakers are often able to catch the addressee's attention when they might not have otherwise. As one Igbo respondent explained:

> The proverb makes somebody think twice. If you use a proverb people might be more likely to take your advice. It has an effect on the other person that literal words may not have. He begins to reconsider. First, he tries to understand the proverb and this puts him in a line of relaxation to think. It becomes food for thought and has an effect on someone's actions.

Quotes with their metaphorical and/or poetic internal structure are also cognitively different from their surrounding context. As the respondent's comment above illustrates, they do not have the ability to divert the addressee's attention from the tension or intensity of interpersonal relations to the enjoyment ("relaxation") of language play. The extent to which the foregrounding nature of quotes affects different aspects of interactional behavior has not yet been fully explored. Obviously, metaphors do force the addressee to process language differently, which again in some cultures may serve to draw the attention of the addressee more so than "ordinary" (non-quoted) language might.

As for Igbo society, and perhaps many other African societies, metaphorical language represents a mental challenge for mature members of the culture. Those who fail to process the language correctly are less skilled and less respected in the society than those who show that they can meet the challenge by responding appropriately. Those who show a lack of intelligence by not responding to the correct interpretation of the quote or proverb are somewhat shamed or embarrassed. As one Igbo proverb puts it: *Atụrụ ilu kà ọ gbà onye nzuzu gharịị.* (L.T. Proverbs are used to confuse stupid people.) The following narrative account illustrates how important the addressee's response to a quote can be.

> Two young men, Obiechina and Ogbuaghu, were friends and often chatted with each other; however, Ogbuaghu and another man, Chilaka, were enemies. Now Chilaka had a reputation in the community as someone who showed off any new things he got. One day when Ogbuaghu and Obiechina were talking with each other in the compound, Chilaka passed by wearing a new pair of shoes which he had just purchased. Obiechina took advantage of the opportunity to insult Chilaka in a very painful way, saying to Ogbuabhu in a voice loud enough for Chilaka to hear: "*Nwatà gotere àkpà ọhụrụ nà-ànya ya were àlabà ụrā.*" (L.T. When a child gets a new bag, he loves it so much that he even sleeps with it.) As a result Chilaka felt highly ridiculed but because he was intelligent enough not to react by quarrelling or fighting and since he could not quickly think of a proverb to counter the insult, he simply muttered something under his breath and walked away.

To summarise, the foregrounding of metaphorical quotes more easily catches the addressee's attention because the quote is associated with a mental challenge by virtue of its "foreignness." In a sense using quotes is a way of putting an addressee on the spot or testing the addressee's knowledge of the ways of the culture and verbal behavior. Those who can quickly respond appropriately and skillfully pass the test with higher marks than those who respond inappropriately--by fighting or quarrelling.

Authoritativeness

Authoritativeness is bestowed on the quote by virtue of its association with the highly respected authorities of the community, the "experts." Specific quotes are chosen according to the orientation of the addressee. The skilled speaker can infer the orientation of his audience and choose quotes accordingly to give his message the maximum authoritativeness. If the orientation is Christian, Biblical quotes are chosen; if the orientation is traditional, Igbo proverbs are chosen; and if the orientation is Western and formally educated, English sayings and proverbs, or better yet, Shakespeare and other classical authors are quoted. In some cases, as a mark of even more skillfulness, bilinguals will use a quote in one language and paraphrase using an equivalent quote from another language. By doing this, they are adding even more authority to their words since they draw on experts from two very different cultures, e.g., traditional Igbo culture and modern Western culture.

Authoritativeness involves two crucial factors. First of all, the quote represents a sort of "community acceptance" (Mukařovský, 1971), i.e., acceptance by the audience of both thought and wording of the proverb. Consequently, the notion of correctness and acceptance as "correct" adds power to the message conveyed. Secondly, the "expert" with whom the quote is associated must be highly respected in the community to which the addressee belongs. A member of Igbo culture explained it this way:

> When you quote, you are saying that what you say should be considered not on the grounds of who is saying it but where it came from. You are speaking in terms of what you have learned from reputed authorities. Quoting is documentation and should be listened to because it comes from a more reputable or higher source.

The degree of authoritativeness of the quote and ultimately the strength of the quote are both determined more by the association with experts than any other property of the quote. The extent to which this is true of all societies remains to be discovered. In European societies this may not be true since there is hardly any connection in proverbs with the originators of the quote. However, for Igbo society the opposite seems to be true. Much of the authoritativeness of proverbs and other quotes rests in the association of the quote with the "experts." One particular proverb refers to this notion: *Otù nwoke sì onye gwàrà ya okwù nà ọ tọ̀rọ̀ ya, ya agwa ya okwū onye tọrọ ya gwàrà ya.* (L.T. A man once said if a person tells him something and claims that it was told to him by his senior, he would quote something from someone who seniored that man.) This quote illustrates the connection between quoting as documentation and the author of the quote. As one Igbo speaker said: ". . . the main fact that you quote experts or give credence to what they are saying--even though they may be wrong--it's the same way that the proverb gives credence to what you are saying."

Proverbs have a great deal of authoritativeness in Igbo society. This is probably so because they are believed to have originated from those who most skillfully followed the traditions of the society, the former elders and the present ancestors. These historical personages are believed to have good "reputations" and are thus associated with good rather than evil spirits. Consequently, proverbs have a touch of sacredness since they are a symbolic means by which the ancestors continue to participate authoritatively in present day Igbo life. The internal aspects of the proverb, such as archaic terms and the like, along with its semantic reference often marks it as stemming from ancestral time and tradition. These qualities are again important in conveying authoritativeness since they remind the speaker that the origin of the proverb was not primarily triggered by aesthetic qualities (poetic values) or even folk wisdom, but rather by a highly respected and skilled expert in the community who first created and utilized them. The following proverb exhibits some archaic semantic reference: Wepụ̀ akā ēnwē n'ófē, nà ọ̀ dị̀ kà akā mmādu. (Remove the hand of a monkey from your stew or it might be taken as a human's hand.) In other words, people might infer you are cooking a human rather than a monkey if you don't remove the monkey's hand. This proverb, incidentally, was told by a female college student to her female married friend who was studying often with other male friends leaving the impression or the interpretation that perhaps she was also having extra-marital relations. Her male friends had become the "monkey's hand" which resembled a "human's hand" causing others to add very different interpretations than perhaps existed. The proverb was quoted to subtly advise a fellow friend of the interpretations of her actions which she may have been totally unaware of. The archaic aspect of the proverb no doubt added some degree of authoritativeness to give it a persuasive communicative effect.

Thus, since the ancestors are believed to have a great deal of power over present day life in Igbo society, the addressee is forced to pay attention and to consider the proverb more so than the words of an ordinary non-expert and less authoritative member of the society. To summarize using the words of one Igbo respondent:

> Using proverbs brings excitement. It's a symbol of those who have had constant contact with the ways of the culture and the customs--someone who grew up with the elders; this then brings them great respect because people respect the elders a lot. When you hear someone using proverbs, you have a lot of respect for him.

Reference to Societal Norms and Values

The quotes used in quoting behavior allude to the values which the society uphold as important and critical. It is these values which the speaker often exhorts or persuades the addressee to accept by using quoting behavior. The semantic reference of the figurative meaning of a metaphorical quote, such as a proverb, refers to values which the community accepts as its guidelines for living. Quoting behavior encourages the maintenance of traditional values by pointing out to individuals in usually non-threatening ways that they have strayed from these values. For example, generosity is a cultural value which is extremely important in Igbo society. One needs only look at the lavishness of parties and the hospitality of hosts towards their guests who may drop in at any time unannounced to understand just how much generosity is valued in most African societies. Members of Igbo society who enjoy the generosity of others but fail to show such generosity in return are often chided with the following proverb, especially when they are in the process of enjoying another's generosity at a party or in other situations: *Òri ǹkè mmàdụ̀, mmàdụ̀ ò nà-èrikwe ǹke ya?* (He who eats other's things, when will others eat his own?). The more general meaning explains how this proverb serves to encourage the maintenance of a significant cultural value: 'Those who enjoy the generosity of others should also give something in return.' Thus, quotes are a means by which the society's values may be perpetuated through interpersonal interaction, for they serve to quote past events symbolic of current values and orientations. The philosophical meaning of one Igbo proverb points this out: *E jị ụkà ème ụkà*. (You use speech in making a speech.) That is, you quote past events for present circumstances.

Just as it is possible to convey the same values using a variety of different proverbs, it is also sometimes possible to convey the same values using a variety of different quotes: English proverbs, English literary quotes or Biblical sayings. Those who are skillful in both English and Igbo can often paraphrase quotes across languages, conveying the same value messages. They also have the versatility of expressing the values desired in the type of quote which is best suited for the addressee or audience involved. The values which the quotes refer to are one of the functional properties which aid the quote in being an effective communicative tool in quoting behavior.

Prestige

Quotes carry a high degree of prestige in Igbo society. This research suggests that prestige not only comes from the internal aspects of the proverb, which make it an aesthetically pleasing genre, and the external aspects, which connect the quote with the experts of tradition, but even more importantly quotes represent the epitomy of skillfulness in the language and ways of the culture. Quoting proverbs is one significant way in which skillfulness in language and the ways of the culture can be displayed. It is this display of skill which yields prestige and value to the user of the proverb who often uses positive persuasion to avoid personal confrontation with another person. This was illustrated in the previous example discussed under the functional property of depersonalization.

Prestige is also awarded, however, to those who seek to defeat an opponent through quotes. In fact, prestige is awarded to those who are skillful enough to use proverbs to appease or to attack. They are a verbal means by which speakers can elevant themselves. Perhaps a common Igbo proverb explains this even better: Ukà bù ṅkà. (Speech is an art.) Philosophically, this means that those who don't know the art of speaking are often misunderstood and embarrassed, whereas those who do know the "art" or skill of speaking receive prestige. Proverbs or quotes are one of the most prestigious forms of speech in Igbo society which explains why they can have such a persuasive or detrimental impact on the addressee(s). In the words of one respondent: "If you use proverbs, people will sit up and say to themselves, 'Oh he has really got something to say and is intelligent.'"

The functional property of prestige also serves as a sort of compliment or praise to the addressee when used to avoid personal confrontation. The fact that the speaker uses a courteous and polite prestigious speech form to criticize the addressee's behavior or attack a sensitive issue puts the addressee in the mood to accept the message without entering into a personal confrontation with the speaker. In fact, it is the prestige property which encourages this acceptance. On the other hand, when used in battle situations, the prestige property serves to help the speaker disgrace the opponent since rather than praising his intelligence this prestigious form of speech--the quote--makes the addressee appear ignorant and unskillful before the audience. In the account that follows Okorie utilizes this opportunity to achieve a little revenge through public disgrace.

> An older male, Oti, did not get along with the relative of another male, Okorie. Because of Oti's offensive actions towards Okorie's close relative, Okorie considered Oti an enemy. He was looking for an opportunity to revenge Oti. One day there was a public meeting where many men in the community had gathered to discuss community matters. Oti stood up and made a suggestion go the group. This suggestion was not very intelligent, especially for a man of his age. Okorie took advantage of this opportunity to insult Oti before the group saying: "Nwatà kwùe okwù, à màrà ka àhụ ta ra." (L.T. When a child speaks, his maturity is portrayed.) That is, Oti had spoken and now everyone knew how stupid he was. Okorie had demeaned Oti in public and Oti felt very insulted and angry, so he tried to counter Okorie's insult with another proverb.

There is another possible source of the prestige functional property. Proverbs are by nature indirect and general statements. Folklore and observations of the ways of Igbo culture suggest that Igbo society places a high value on the indirect and less obvious as opposed to the direct and obvious.[17] In fact it is in this ability to be indirect and less obvious on which the cultural notion of "intelligence" (àmàmihe) rests. Proverbs are just one tool of indirection. By inference, part of their prestige is derived from the cultural appreciation of indirectness. In fact the Igbo folk conception of "intelligence" includes: 1) knowing and applying the laws of the land in a skillful manner and 2) being able to use the appropriate strategies to achieve one's goal. Quoting proverbs reflects skill in both. As one Igbo respondent phrased it: "The common language any fool can go about it, but the use of proverbs displays your intelligence and maturity in that language and experience."

NOTES

1. In 1961, after two or three different orthographies had been introduced and used for written Igbo, a commission (The Onwu Commission) appointed by the Eastern Regional Government recommended an official orthography for the Igbo language. Today this orthography is accepted as the standard orthography and used in most written material. The Onwu Orthography is therefore utilized in this study. This orthography uses an eight vowel system which accords with the Igbo phonemic system very well. Ladefoged (1964) divides the Igbo vowel system according to front vs. back and pharyngeal constriction vs. lack of pharyngeal constriction. The chart below illustrates the vowel system in the Onwu Orthography with phonemic equivalents in / /. The four vowels with [+pharyngeal constriction] harmonize as do the four vowels with [-pharyngeal constriction]. Vowel harmony usually occurs within lexical units and between pronouns and most verbal forms.

VOWELS

	ị /I/	i /i/
Front	a /a/	e /e/
Back	ọ /ɔ/	o /o/
	ụ /ʊ/	u /u/
	+	−

Pharyngeal Constriction

The Consonants in the Onwu Orthography include: b, ch, d, f, g, gb, gh, gw, h, j, k, kp, kw, l, m, n, nw, ny, p, r, s, sh, t, v, w, y, z.

Igbo is a tonal language with a "terraced level" tonal system (Welmers, 1973: 82). In Welmer's (loc. cit., 84-86) analysis (which is used in this study) Igbo has three tonemes: high, low, and stop. These three tones are marked as follows:

    High tone = unmarked
    Low tone = \
    Step tone = - (never sentence initial and only when immediately following a high tone)

2. L.T. refers to a literal translation of the proverb, that is its most obvious meaning despite the context in which it is used.

3. P.T. refers to a philosophical translation of the proverb. This type of translation was elicited from language usage knowledge of traditional and experienced members of Igbo culture who interpreted the most common meaning of the proverb in a broad sense. P.T. is the metaphorical level of meaning. In some cases, philosophical translations are given in this work to help the reader understand more clearly the cultural meaning ascribed by Igbos to a literal translation.

4. <u>Igbo</u> is the term used to refer to a group of people who identify with one another and speak mutually comprehensible dialects of the same language--Igbo. <u>Igbo</u> was previously spelled <u>Ibo</u> as written by Europeans who made no distinction between the phonemes /b/ and /ɓ/-- an implosive spelled as <u>gb</u> in the Onwu Orthography--which are part of the Igbo language.

Because of wide variations in customs and other cultural patterns among the Igbo which may be attributed to their decentralized nature in part, this study deals only with one major group which shares a common history and political background, the Owerri Igbo.

5. The distinction of proverbs as quoting behavior is owed to Jan Mukařovský, a literary specialist of the Prague school. For a translation of the portion of his book dealing with proverbs, see the Appendix.

6. The "ethnography of communication" refers to an interactional approach to language behavior (Gumperz, 1972: 5) which seeks to understand the following: (1) the means of speaking available to the members of a speech community, e.g., speech codes, speech acts, genres, etc,; (2) the community ground rules for speaking, i.e. the norms, strategies, and values; (3) the native contexts of speech activity, i.e. speech events, situations, scenes, etc,; and (4) verbal art in the framework of social situations for particular cultures (Bauman and Sherzer, 1974).

7. <u>Ordinary</u> refers to other speech acts which do not use proverbs

but may express a similar notion or idea.

8. <u>Interactional setting</u> is used in place of more colloquial and ambiguous terms, such as, <u>context</u> or <u>situation</u>. In this study, <u>interactional setting</u> refers to the setting for a flow of interaction between one or more participants in face-to-face contact which is bounded in time and place and defined by the members of the culture. The interactional setting includes all the various aspects of the actual interactional flow, e.g., interlocutors, audience, physical setting, psychological climate, purpose of the interaction, intended effect, and speech acts utilized.

9. I owe the term "folk verbal account" to Mathiot who distinguishes three types of folk verbal accounts which can serve as data for analysis: (1) recollections, (2) immediate recalls, and (3) blow-by-blow commentaries. For more information on these different types of verbal accounts see Mathiot, 1976.

10. The "immediate function" refers to the observable role of a certain behavioral system in the lives of the users which may be more immediately recognizable. This function can be ascertained at a fairly low level of abstraction (Mathiot and Garvin, 1975).

The "ultimate function" refers to the deeper significance a particular role of language may play in the lives of the speakers. It is ascertained on a fairly high level of abstraction in analysis.

I owe both concepts to a functionalist view of language as interpreted by Garvin and Mathiot. (See Garvin, 1977).

11. The functional empiricist view of language holds that functions should be inferred from the observation of behavior on several levels of abstraction rather than postulated in advance (Garvin, 1977).

12. <u>Ordinary speech</u> refers to other speech acts which do not quote but may express the same notion or idea.

13. Quotes differ from ordinary speech in that their internal structure is fairly frozen, i.e., they do not permit rearrangement of units or substitution of lexical items. The quote is very much like an idiom in that its internal units combine to make a semantic reference yet the alteration of any of these units may alter either the semantic reference or its lexical status as a quote.

For more information on aspects of the internal structure of proverbs, see Emenanjọ, 1972:109-114.

14. Igbo has a third person impersonal pronoun which may be realized as [a] or [e] since it harmonizes with the vowel of the verb stem:

à	ga	ghī	"People did not go" or "one did not go."
pron.	go	neg.	
	or		
è	je -	ghī	"People did not go" or "one did not go."
pron.	go	neg.	

Other linguistic devices which make the proverb impersonal include:
(1) the use of a noun classifier *onye* ("one who"); (2) the use of
a nominalization, achieved simply by tonal alteration of a verb, e.g.
ójì oso--"one who rushes"; and (3) the use of animals or objects as
subjects of the sentence.

15. Foregrounding, somewhat akin to Mukarovsky's notion of "deauto-
matization" (Mukařovský, 1977, 1978), does not refer to any poetic
or aesthetic quality here but rather as simply a sharp contrast in
internal structure (phonological, syntactical, and semantic) from
the linguistic context surrounding the quote. Foregrounding occurred
in two different types of linguistic contexts in my data: (1) discourse or narrative contexts and (2) interactional contexts. This
book discusses only the latter.

16. As a participant observater in Igbo society, I observed an Igbo
Roman Catholic priest who was well-liked by his villager parishioners
because he often quoted Igbo proverbs when he spoke to them. Reali-
zing that their orientation was traditional, he often conveyd
Christian messages and values by quoting Igbo proverbs. The ability
to do this gained him the respect he needed to persuade his audience
to accept Christianity.

17. Several less prestigious means of verbal indirection are prevalent in Igbo society. For example, *ikpē ìkpè* or "speaking in general
statements" refers to this. This term includes making general statements which may be metaphorical, idiomatic or even proverbial which
refer indirectly to others who are present. *Imé àkàjà*--using words
carelessly or freely--by using forms similar as in *ikpē ìkpè* but
without circumspection. Folktales are another verbal means of indirection as well as satire used in women's song and dance (Nwoga,
1971: 34).

CHAPTER 2
STUDYING QUOTING BEHAVIOR

THEORY OF THE USE OF PROVERBS

To date, although there have been numerous accounts of proverbs by folklorists along with lists and translations of proverbs, there has been little to no discussion regarding a theoretical foundation for proverbial use. One of the very few authors who has ever dealt in depth with this problem was Jan Mukařovský, a literary scholar of the Prague school in Czechslovakia. Since his comments of theoretical interest to the study of proverbs exist only in Czech, a translation of crucial segments is provided in Appendix B of this book. It is interesting to note that many of his observations are parallel to the few comments made by investigators of diverse African societies using proverbs. Thus, Mukařovský's theoretical frame of reference has been extensively used in the research cited in this book.

Mukařovský's Theory of Proverbs

Mukařovský (1971: 297) places proverbs in a more comprehensive framework than researchers of African proverbs. He views the use of proverbs as a manifestation of quoting behavior in that there is a feeling that a "foreign subject" (third party) has intruded into the "context." Although Mukařovský focuses on the proverb, it can be assumed that there are other manifestations of quoting behavior in some societies, e.g. scholarly quotes, Biblical quotes, literary quotes, and perhaps one might also include advertising jingles or slogans.

As the Appendix B indicates, Mukařovský distinguishes several traits that define proverbs as one manifestation of quoting behavior. In regard to "context," he points out that quotes stand out in the "context" and also merge with it (Mukařovský, 1971:298).

That is, they are a different form of speech than the utterances which surround them and consequently are instantly marked as unique or different; yet they have little or no existence without this "context." The unique interdependence of the proverb and its "context" is summed up by Mukařovský (loc. cit., 299) in his observation that a quote may have the value of an allusion or euphemism and thus: "A quotation may often serve to indicate something that the speaker for whatever reason does not wish to say out directly."

A second characteristic of quotes noted by Mukařovský is crucial to the study of proverbs in African societies. This is their evaluative potential when used as "addressed speech" or rhetorical tools. Mukařovský (loc. cit., 300) points out that in "addressed speech" a value judgment is achieved not by the nature of the quote or proverb itself so much as by the user or citer of the proverb who, playing the role of evaluator, "takes a certain position to the matter at hand by virtue of the use of the quote and exhorts the listener to take that same position." The awareness that the user or speaker of the proverb is not the author or creator can strengthen the message conveyed. Mukařovský (loc. cit., 302) refers to this as "theatricalization." As explained by Mukařovský and researchers of African literature and folklore, the presence of an evaluative element is one of the fundamental characteristics of the proverb and its use. It is through this "addressed speech" that a proverb or quote permits the intrusion of a third party into the interactional setting who sort of "speaks through the mouth of the speaker" (loc. cit., 300).

Since the proverb "in its context [interactional setting] is perceived as a synonym which replaces a more direct expression" (loc. cit., 340) and is considered an authoritatively valid utterance, in "addressed speech" the speaker can strongly convey a value judgment for which he is not held responsible and which can also have persuasive impact on the addressee(s). In quoting behavior then, the degree of strength felt by the participants in the interactional setting is influenced by the depersonalized nature of the form of speech and its use as well as the group's perception of the authorities from whom this form of speech is derived.

The primary property which proverbs share with other manifestations of quoting behavior is the feeling of a third-party intrusion which enables the user of the proverb to play the role of evaluator and attempt to persuade the addressee and/or audience to take a similar position to the matter at hand. However, other features of the proverb can be distinguished which may not be shared with other manifestations of quoting behavior. Mukařovský (loc. cit., 293) divides the features of the proverb into three groups: (1) those characterizing the proverb with regard to its surrounding interactional setting; (2) those characterizing the relation between the proverb and the "subject" (speaker); and (3) those characterizing the internal semantic structure of the proverb itself. The first two sets of features are externally defined and the last set of features are internally defined.

In his discussion of features characterizing the proverb with
regard to its interactional setting, Mukařovský (loc. cit., 285)
notes: ". . . the proverb lives . . . a complete life only in
context." Even though the proverb is felt to be an integral part
of its interactional setting, it is also felt to be a foreign
element. In African proverbs, at least, the foreignness is probably
derived from internal aspects of the proverb, e.g. archaic lexicon,
rhythm, and grammatical structure, which differ from ordinary
speech. As mentioned previously, the meaning of the proverb is
ambiguous without its surrounding interactional setting. The interactional setting, however, can quite substantially change the
semantic basis of the proverb (loc. cit., 287).

The features of most interest here are those characterizing the
relation between the proverb and the user which results in "desubjectivization" (depersonalization). By this Mukařovský is referring to the fact that the speaker or citer of the proverb is not
the creator or author of the proverb. Mukařovský connects this
"desubjectivization" with three properties: the traditional nature
of the proverb, the community acceptance, and the feeling of the
presence or interference of a third party into the interactional
setting. By traditional nature is meant a symbol of the values
which extend beyond the interactional setting in which a proverb
is used and also the frozen wording or unchangeable nature of the
proverb. The traditional nature offers strong advantages to the
speaker. "Using a proverb sometimes the speaker can escape being
under the control of reality which would be in conflict with the
assertion that he has made by using a proverb" (loc. cit., 294).
Thus, the speaker can avoid being directly responsible or obligated
for the message conveyed and can save himself embarrassment. This
notion conforms to Nwoga's (1975) comment about the indirectness
of proverbs in certain interactional settings in Igbo society and
the resulting effect of saving both speaker and addressee embarrassment. Nwoga (1975: 198-201) categorizes the use of proverbs
into two basic usages: (1) the "illuminative usage" which basically consists of using the quote to reinforce one's message; and (2)
"corrective usage" which basically consists of indirect comments on
behavior with the intent to correct.

The second property noted by Mukařovský (1971: 295) which he views
as connected with "desubjectivization," is "community acceptance."
By this he means that there is a societal acceptance or consensus
as to the notions expressed in the proverbs. In explaining just
where this consensus derives from, Mukařovský maintains that this
consensus is ". . . linked to the attitude that the perceiver has
with regard to the proverb." (Mukařovský 1971: 295). However,
Mukařovský fails to consider that this "community acceptance" may
in turn be derived from recognition or association with the author
or creator of the proverb. Nevertheless, this seems to be the case
with African proverbs. It is this association with the author
which often can determine the degree of strength the proverb holds
in the society. For example, in African societies where proverbs
are believed to have been created by the ancestors or famous historical personages, proverbs carry great strength because these

societies attach a high value to the ancestors. The African attitude seems slightly different from the attitude towards proverbs in European societies where proverbs are considered to have anonymous authors and are viewed as pieces of folk wisdom.

The third property which Mukařovský mentions as fundamental to this "desubjectivization" is the feeling that someone other than the speaker has entered into the interactional setting. This property was discussed in detail previously.

The third set of features of proverbs noted by Mukařovský are those characterizing the internal semantic structure of the proverb itself. These include the following characteristics: the generalizing meanings of proverbs; the norm creating and evaluative nature of proverbs; and the figurativeness of the meaning of the proverbs (loc. cit., 305). A characteristic of the internal semantic structure of the proverb which is crucial to this study is that the proverb in its interactional setting serves to replace a more direct expression (loc. cit., 340).

FUNDAMENTAL ASSUMPTIONS

This investigation of quoting behavior in Igbo society follows the descriptive approach in the context of the "ethnography of speaking." Quoting behavior as exemplified in the use of proverbs in Igbo society provides the opportunity to investigate directly the use of language as an aspect of human social behavior in general, and verbal behavior in particular.

It is assumed in this research that a complex notion of function as explained by Mathiot and Garvin (1975) can serve to explain analytically observations of quoting behavior. Function is defined as the significant role that an aspect of behavior plays in the life of the people utilizing it. Therefore, the focus of the research reported on in this book is on external functioning or rather how the system of quoting behavior works in everyday lives of the speakers. In uncovering the external function emphasis is placed on both the apparent and less apparent roles of quoting behavior.

This work begins with the following basic assumptions which represent the basic beliefs about human social behavior held by the researcher which are directly relevant to the study of quoting behavior.

> Assumption I. Culture is a schema for understanding
> the world

This assumption does not refer to any psychological or physiological mechanism but rather to a way to look at culture which anthropologists, like Redfield, have termed "outlook on life" or world view, i.e. "the way people see themselves in relation to all else." As mentioned previously, Opler (1945) refers to this as "theme." Redfield (1963: 84) succinctly explains this as "how everything looks to a people . . . conceptions of what ought to be as well as what is." (Kluckhohn (1949: 357) spells this notion out in detail:

> There is much more to social and cultural phenomena than immediately meets the ear and eye. . . Each different way of life makes its own assumptions about the ends and purposes of human existence, about ways by which knowledge may be obtained, about the organization of the pigeon holes in which each sense datum is filed, about what human beings have a right to expect from each other and the gods, about what constitutes fulfillment or frustration. Some of these assumptions are made explicit in the lore of the folk; others are tacit premises which the observer must infer by finding consistent trends in word and deed.

The effect of these themes or world view on human social behavior was summarized by Bateson as noted in Kluckhohn (ibid.): "Man . . . constantly imposes on his environment his own constructions and meanings; these constructions and meanings are characteristic of one culture as opposed to another."

This notion of cultural themes is not intended by the investigator as a deep philosophical notion but as recognition that members of the culture live in terms of ideal models which enable them to handle the complexity of reality by distinguishing the relevant from the irrelevant.

Assumption II: Speaking, or the use of language, is patterned within each society in culture-specific ways

Bauman and Sherzer in The Ethnography of Speaking (1975: 30) cite a similar assumption as fundamental to the ethnography of speaking which they define as "concerned with the cultural rules by which social use and nonuse of language is organized." Their interest goes beyond the traditional relativistic statement that all languages and all members of the culture are equally capable of achieving any communicative goal. They point out that not all languages are used for the same communicative purposes and all members of a particular culture are not equally skilled in all uses of the language.

Assumption II is also based on the observation and personal experience that to be able to skillfully communicate in a different language, one has to know not only the correct linguistic forms but also how to use them appropriately, i.e. skilled speakers have knowledge of the variables of the interactional setting, social meaning, and value of particular forms over others.

Assumption III: Factors affecting the social use of language are anchored both in the structure of the society and the particular interactional settings

This assumption is based on the everyday observation and experience that in any given interaction, one is both a member of the society as well as a participant in the specific interactional situation. The <u>use of language</u> refers to both factors. Sociologists make a similar distinction between small groups, which are defined by face-to-face contact, and large groups, which are constituted independent of face-to-face contact (Mathiot and Garvin, 1975: 153). The assumption made here is that both settings or groups must be dealt with to interpret adequately the social patterning of quoting behavior.

<u>Assumption IV: Proverbs can be clearly distinguished from other forms of speech</u>

This assumption is based on observations regarding the nature of quotes as well as the nature of their use which clearly separate quoting behavior from other types of verbal behavior. There are two attributes which commonly distinguish quotes, whether they be citations from religious books such as the Bible, the Torah, or the Koran, or proverbs or literary quotes. First, quotes have clearly marked boundaries which neatly delineate their beginning and their end. Secondly, members of the culture have a high degree of awareness of them. The majority of the studies on proverbs in various African cultures have related to one of these two attributes. The first attribute has yielded studies which treated proverbs as entities in their own right and explicated such things as poetic style, rhythm, and phonological devices such as tone. The second attribute has yielded lists of proverbs from numerous cultures with some sort of translation for each in a philosophical or literal sense.

Assumption IV is based on the observation that in terms of the nature of their use, proverbs have three characteristic attributes: (1) they are commonly introduced in clear-cut ways, i.e. with <u>introducers</u> such as, "it is said that"; "our people say"; "one Igbo proverb says"; or "as our ancestors said"; (2) they are flexible in usage; and (3) their specific social meaning can only be interpreted using the specific interactional setting in which they occur.

The second attribute, flexibility, refers to the observation that the same proverb can be used in a variety of different situations with different meanings and purposes. It is this attribute which has confused attempts to classify lists of proverbs. Those who have attempted to categorize their list most often use cosmological themes through which several proverbs are related, e.g."generosity" or "shame", etc. (Ogbalu, 1965).

The third attribute, i.e., the importance of the interactional setting in interpreting the meaning of the proverb, relates to the notion of "field-derived" and "system-derived" characteristics explained by Bühler, a member of the Linguistic Circle of Prague, in his theory of language. Bühler's "system-derived" characteristics refer to certain "informational" characteristics which are inherent to a speech sign or form of speech." (Garvin, 1966: 213). In our study, "system-derived" refers to the constant meaning which proverbs have independent of the interactional settings in which they may occur. "Field-derived" characteristics refer to those characteristics which the speech sign or form of speech obtain as a result of the interaction between it and the surrounding field (or interactional setting in the case of proverbs) [Ibid.] In our study, "field-derived" characteristics of proverbs refer to the variation in meaning in different interactional settings. Bühler's conception thus adds the insight that "between a form and its context there is not merely an incidental relation of adjacency, but an organic connection of fundamental functional-significance" (loc. cit., 215). Using Bühler's conception, the second attribute of "flexibility" can be viewed as a wide variety of "field-derived" variation, and the crucial importance of the third attribute is underscored.

Assumption V: Proverbs have both internal structure and external functioning and the two are integrally related

This assumption refers to what Hymes called the integral relation between communicative form and function (Hymes, 1964). Garvin (1977: 18) has referred to this as the form-function co-variance. As such, this assumption derives from a structural-functional theory of language which claims that language has both structure and function and that each can serve as an object of study in its own right. Structure refers to the pattern and organization of the linguistic forms while function refers to how these forms relate to aspects of man's social life as revealed by their usage.

Emenanjo (1972) suggests that Igbo quotes are characterized by different clausal constructions, a rhythmic patterning of phrases, and various poetic devices, e.g., repetition, contrast, and alliteration. Obviously, the internal structure of proverbs serves to set them off from ordinary language.

The less obvious observation is that the attributes of the internal structure mentioned above are fundamental to the functioning of quoting behavior. Nwoga (1975: 192) has noted that the necessary terseness and attributes of the internal structure of proverbs, e.g., rhythm and tonal structure, facilitates memorization. This is essential in the case of proverbs, which are commonly utilized as references to wisdom and knowledge in oral societies. These observations support the notion of an integral relation between internal structure and external functioning.

Assumption VI: The external function of quoting behavior in Igbo society can be inferred from folk conceptions offered by Igbo speakers through guided recall and hypothetical cases

It is assumed by the investigator that in order to understand social behavior and specifically the use of proverbs, it is necessary to obtain folk conceptions regarding the aspects of interactional settings in which they occur. Folk conceptions are essentially the beliefs of what is and what should be as revealed by the members of the culture. Some social scientists refer to these folk conceptions as ideal models of behavior. In this research, folk conceptions are assumed to underlie aspects of observable behavior in actual interactional events of the members of a culture which reveal how members of the culture view the use of proverbs; their norms of expectation; and value judgments.

There are two major implications of Assumption VI. The first refers to the treatment of these data. It seems only sensible that in order to get an inside view or a notion of the ideal models that members of the culture use to screen "what is and what ought to be" out of an array of actual behavior, data should be gathered from the members of the culture themselves. This information regarding the _inside_ view cannot be obtained only from the observations of overt behavior by a non-native member of the culture. In order to arrive at these ideal models, ethnographic interviews can reveal useful information regarding: (1) what the members of the culture talk about; (2) how they talk about it; and (3) what they remember from past situations or foresee in future situations.

The second major implication is that since the inside view or the native's point of view and the objective view arrived at by the non-native analyst are necessarily different in nature, data regarding folk conceptions obtained from members of the culture should be treated separately from data obtained from observation of actual events by the researcher.

FIELD METHODS

Initially a pilot study was conducted to define the problem and design an appropriate methodology for most efficiently collecting data regarding the problem. The pilot study revealed two key notions regarding proverbs: (1) the most important requirement which proverbs must fulfill is appropriateness to the interactional setting; and (2) the degree of status which a speaker can achieve depends upon his skill in the use of quotes such as proverbs. Thus, the problem was defined as discovering those factors which could account for _appropriateness_ and _skill_ as defined by Igbo speakers.

The following types of data were utilized in this research: (1) interpretations of previous observed overt behavior in which proverbs were used as witnessed by both the researcher and the respondent: (2) recall of past or hypothetical interactional settings in which proverbs were utilized; (3) interpretations of recalled past or hypothetical interactional settings in which proverbs were utilized; (4) detailed information regarding various aspects of the Owerri Igbo way of life; and (5) folk terms and folk explanations of Igbo speech event; (6) records of participant observation made by the investigator and (7) tape-recordings of interactional settings in which proverbs were used spontaneously, e.g., meetings, kola sharing ceremonies, sacred rituals, competitions, and public ceremonies.[1]

Most of the data base consisted of type 3 materials which were tape-recorded during informal interviewing sessions of approximately one hour each, using "guided recall" methodology.[2] Such sessions most typically included two or more respondents and were carried out in English. The tape-recorded interviews were later transcribed by the investigator and utilized in typewritten form for analysis. Table 1 lists those questions which were utilized in the field to collect the major type of data for the data base.

SAMPLE

Respondents consisted of adult male and female Igbo-speakers most of whom were bilingual in Igbo and English and all of whom were knowledgeable in the use of proverbs. The fieldwork sites were in two different parts of the former Owerri Province: (1) Alvan Ikoku College of Education in Owerri township; and (2) Uturu village-group (town) which is located near Okigwe township (see Figure 1). There were 35 respondents from the first fieldwork site. They came from various villages in the former Owerri Province area. Twenty-five respondents were drawn from the second fieldwork site and were all members of the Uturu community.

Most respondents from both fieldwork sites were Igbo-English bilinguals; therefore, type 1 data were collected in English. A few respondents had limited-to-no knowledge of English. In such cases, type 1 data were collected in Igbo along with simultaneous translation into English by other bilingual members of Igbo society.

It should be noted that for the sake of simplicity and uniformity in the data, proverbs are written in the Owerri dialect of Igbo using the orthography of the Onwu Commission.[3]

Table I. Follow-up Questions Used For
Ethnographic Interviewing

Interactional Event

1. Where does the proverb occur in the interactional event?

2. What goes on before the proverb is used?

3. What happens or can possibly happen after the proverb is used?

Interactional Scene

1. What are the physical aspects of the interactional event? (Where does the interaction take place?)

2. What is the psychological climate? (anger, fun, serious, light)

Table I.--continued

Participants (Speaker, addressee, audience)

1. What is the possible relationship of speaker to addressee? (friends, enemies, same/different status positions)
2. How many people may be present?
3. What previous information is necessary to understand the proverb? (e.g., reputation of speaker or addressee)
4. Who could not say this to whom? (wife to husband, younger to older male, child to mother, junior to senior)

Speaker Intention

1. Why does the speaker use this proverb?
2. What does the speaker want to achieve?
3. How does the speaker want the addressee to feel as a result of the proverb he uses?
4. Why is a proverb used rather than ordinary speech?

Effect: Outcome

1. What is the psychological impact (effect) of the proverb on the addressee? on the audience? on the speaker himself?
2. Is the effect that which was intended by speaker?
3. How would you feel if someone said this to you in a similar situation?
4. How does this effect differ from the effect ordinary or direct language would have had?

Response of Addressee

1. In what different ways can the addressee respond?
2. Why does he/she respond in these ways?

Table I.--continued

	Function
1.	What is the function of the proverb in this interaction? (Could you explain more what you mean?)
2.	Why does the speaker perform this function?
3.	What does the speaker want to achieve in the long run by saying this?

To make interviewing sessions more personal and informal, these questions were not asked in the same order as listed above nor literally, but rather were paraphrased and embedded in informal conversation.

Fig. 1. Map of Igbo-speaking area

ANALYSIS

Further ethnographic interviewing regarding conflict revealed that conflict is perceived by members of Igbo society as a series of stages which get progressively more serious and which are consequently handled differently. A flow chart of the process of conflict development was constructed to use as a cultural frame of reference for the classification of interactional settings represented in type 1 data (Appendix C). The progression of the conflict was used as a framework within which type 1 material could be classified and analyzed. Thus each different interactional setting in which a proverb is used can be defined as one point in the flow of conflict development. Once this specific frame of reference was arrived at, it was possible to classify and analyze particular examples of interaction according to the point in the conflict sequence at which they occur and to infer the factors which could explain the use of proverbs in conflict situations. Thus the analysis led to the major goal of the entire research: a description and interpretation of the role of proverbs in Igbo society as well as the interactional and societal functions which proverbs serve in Igbo society.

NOTES

1. Folk terms are those terms frequently used by the members of the culture to refer to qualities, actions, events, or objects. Folk explanations are definitions or interpretations offered by members of the culture to describe folk terms.

2. "Guided recall" is a technique which prompts the interviewee to recall a past event or a hypothetical event and then describe it in detail. Initially the interviewee is allowed, without interruption, to describe those things which he conceives as important. This is done to encourage the respondent to mention those things he perceives as most important and thus minimize ethnocentric bias on the part of the interviewer. After this description is given, the interviewer then explores, through more detailed questioning, specific aspects of the event which are relevant to his particular research.

3. There is presently no single standard for Igbo. Through the years two major varieties of Igbo have developed--neither is typical of any particular township area, but both represent former sociopolitical strongholds: Owerri Igbo representing most of the area included under the former Owerri Province, and Onitsha Igbo representing most of the area included under the former Onitsha Province. The Owerri dialect was promoted by Protestant religious groups who devoted much time and effort to fostering literacy in Igbo. Today this is the variety most commonly used in writing and most commonly promoted as the Standard for Igbo. The Onitsha dialect was supported by Catholic religious groups who spent less time and energy on literacy. However, this variety of Igbo was the first to be used for printed materials since it originated in the province where political power, money, and printing presses existed. The old Onitsha Province was the first Igbo area to have contact with the Western world's religion and economy as early as 1857. At the beginning of Western contact in religion and government, missionaries

sent church evangelists--who were usually members of Igbo culture native to Onitsha Province--to other parts of Igboland, e.g. parts of Owerri Province. Also, British civil servants did not know Igbo and therefore relied on members of Igbo culture who came from Onitsha Province and naturally spoke the Onitsha variety of Igbo to act as government workers (interpreters, court clerks, and court messengers) throughout Igboland. All of these indigenous groups helped to expose non-Onitsha parts of Igboland to the Onitsha variety of Igbo. In addition, the very first religious and school materials were printed in Onitsha dialect and used all over Igboland.

All of the popularity and influence of Onitsha dialect throughout Igboland diminished with the recommendation of Ida Ward (representative of the School of Oriental and African Studies) in 1939 that Owerri dialect, which she referred to as "Central Igbo," form the basis for Standard Igbo. Immediately following this recommendation, a Translation Bureau was set up to spread this dialect form and a New Orthography was also introduced. From then on, "Central Igbo" or Igbo spoken throughout former Owerri Province became accepted by writers, publishers, and educational authorities for use in the schools.

Since this study is limited to the former Owerri Province area of Igboland, proverbs will be written in the Owerri dialect.

CHAPTER 3
ETHNOGRAPHY OF QUOTING BEHAVIOR

INTRODUCTION

The following ethnographic profile explicates those factors of the social structure in Igbo society which are deemed relevant to the study of quoting behavior. More specifically, the profile focuses on information regarding conflict in Igbo society and how it is managed.

As mentioned previously, since the respondents were all original inhabitants of Owerri Province, only this particular geographic section of Igbo society will be discussed. The term Owerri Igbo is used here in the broadest sense rather than in its more narrow sense. It, therefore, does not refer to only those communities surrounding Owerri Township or only the inhabitants of Owerri Township. In some traditional respects the Owerri Igbo contrast with the Onitsha Igbo and, in fact, clearly makes these distinctions themselves. To what extent this contrast affects the actual usage of quotes, such as proverbs, remains to be discovered.

The description of the social structure offered here is only a brief survey rather than a detailed analysis.[1] It mentions only those aspects of the social structure which are significant and essential to the problem being treated in this investigation. It also focuses on the common aspects of the communities of Owerri Igbo society as opposed to variations from one community to another. For a more detailed analysis and more detailed information regarding variation from one community to another, other ethnographic sources should be consulted.

THE SETTING

The entire Igbo society has a population of about nine million persons organized into some 200 autonomous village-groups in southeastern Nigeria between the Niger River and the Cross River (Ottenberg, 1968: 9). This area is primarily tropical rain forest. The Owerri Igbo inhabit the southeastern part of this area. Today the Owerri Igbo inhabit most of the political division of Imo State. Although no up-to-date statistics could be found regarding the population of the Owerri Igbo, they probably number about five million or more. Residing in a primarily rural environment, the Owerri Igbo have one of the highest population densities in all of Africa. About thirty years ago, it was estimated that their population density was more than 1,000 persons per square mile (Forde and Scott, 1946: 42). The extent to which this high population density has influenced the forms of social groupings and reactions to European contact among the Owerri Igbo remains to be studied. The high population density may, however, offer one explanation for the common occurrence of conflicts and tension in Owerri Igbo speaking communities.

The highest political unit of the rural Owerri Igbo is the village-group, which consists of a cluster of villages.[2] The village-group may range in size from several thousand to over seventy-five thousand persons (Forde and Jones, 1950). Each village-group has a name, an internal organization, and a common meeting place *(ebe nzūkọ)* which serves at once as a ritual, political and marketing centre (Uchendu, 1965; Forde and Jones, 1950; Meek, 1937).

Each village belongs to a village-group and consists of a group of persons living in a single settlement area who hold a common identity regardless of descent ties. The basic units of the village consist of one or more patrilineages *(ụmụ nnà)* which may or may not claim common descent but which together own land and pass on valuable property to males through inheritance.[3] Villages range in population from 40 to 8,000 persons; the average probably includes about 4,500 persons (Forde and Jones, 1950: 17). Each village has a great deal of internal autonomy so that internal disputes are usually handled internally. Each village also has a common meeting place *(mbara)* where social and ritual activities take place.

The patrilineage is the basic social unit of the Owerri Igbo. Each patrilineage is subject to the authority of its ancestors and its lineage head *(onye ji ọfọ)* who holds a sacred staff *(ọfọ)* symbolizing the authority of the ancestors *(nnà nnà)* and who acts as intermediary between the lineage and its ancestors.[4] Each patrilineage in the village shares one or more distinct and densely populated living quarters called *èzi* (compounds). A compound is both a residential and a social unit. Physically, compound refers to the area occupied by the houses of several family members, surrounded by a mud wall with a small house *(òbi)* at the gate entrance where sacrifices are made and where members of the compound assemble. Socially, a compound is a group of lineage members residing together who are subject to the authority of the compound head *(onye isi ezi)*. The size of the compounds varies. Nowadays, a compound usually consists of a small unit of male siblings, their wives, and their children, or several such groups related patrilineally. In this study, nuclear family is used to refer to a family unit consisting of a husband, one wife and the children of the two. A polygynous unit then consists of several nuclear families. A compound, thus, consists of one or more nuclear families related patrilineally. Formerly, an entire patrilineage resided in one compound; nowadays, this same size patrilineage may occupy as many as ten separate compounds.[5] Irrespective of the size of a compound, the eldest male child, and his nuclear family (families) is (are) expected to share the same compound with his father so that he can assist his father and even take over his role when his father dies.

A nuclear family consists of the husband, one wife, and their children. Traditionally, polygyny received prestige and respect in the society because it symbolized wealth. Today, polygyny is becoming less common and has lost some of its prestige.[6] Whether the family is monogomous or polygynous, the wife (wives) is (are) subject to the authority of the husband. In polygynous families, the first wife--irrespective of her age--has seniority over the other wives and receives certain privileges that the other wives do not receive, e.g., choice of parts of the chicken being eaten. However, the first wife has little delegated authority over the other wives. Children of the same father (ųmų̀ di) are subject to the authority of their father and also to the authority of any one of the wives of the father. Co-wives are in constant competition with one another and commonly have conflicts which arise from joint activities with the husband or quarrels between their children. Therefore, when the husband dies, co-wives often split off and live in separate compounds with their unmarried daughters, sons, and the nuclear families of their sons.

Figure 2 (see following page) illustrates the network of social relationships and "social sentiments" typical of the Owerri Igbo.[7] These distinctions are important frames of reference in which <u>social roles</u> and <u>status positions</u> involving conflict can be explained.[8] Figure 2 illustrates the concentric relationship of these groups as well as the distance of one group to another. In general the social "structural distance" (Evans-Pritchard, 1940: 110) between individuals, both in terms of residence and degree of social interaction, is correlated with descent: the nearer the members are genealogically, the closer the social relationship. Thus, the social relations between members of the same social unit are much closer and more intimate than those between members of different social units. For example, members of the same kin group are a closer unit than members of non-kin groups and are expected to protect each other and maintain solidarity more than non-kin groups. Members of a nuclear family (families) owe these same obligations to each other to a stronger degree than to non-nuclear family members of the same kin group. This is explained in more detail below (see Network of Social Relationships).

Case Example

The hierarchy of membership units to which an Owerri Igbo belongs can be illustrated by a case example based on a respondent for this investigation, Nwachukwu. Nwachukwu has two wives and several unmarried children. He has provided a house for each wife as well as

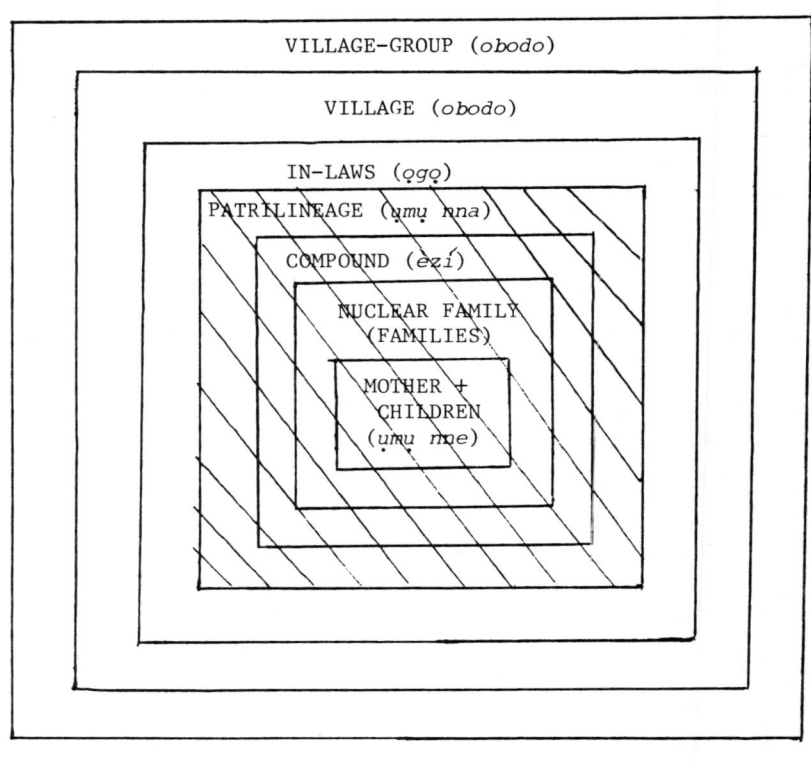

Fig. 2. Hierarchy of social units among the Owerri Igbo

for himself. His first wife has three male children ages 5, 10, and 12. She feeds and clothes all three but only the youngest continues to sleep in her house. The other two sleep in their father's house. The second wife has two daughters ages 4 and 11. Both sleep in the house of their mother. Nwachukwu's father is dead. His mother is living and shares the compound with him. Nwachukwu and his nuclear families share the compound with his three brothers and their nuclear families. His sisters are married, and therefore do not live in the compound with their brothers but rather in the compounds of their husbands. Two of the sisters do not even live in the same village. All three sisters come to visit Nwachukwu's compound very often.

Since Nwachukwu is the eldest living son of his father, and the eldest male in the compound, he functions as head of the compound. Nwachukwu's compound is one of eight compounds which are occupied by all of his living relatives related by blood (patrilineage). The patrilineage is named Umu-okudele and is headed by Obinna, the eldest living male of Umu-okudele, who is Nwachukwu's father's brother. No members of Umu-okudele are allowed to have sexual relations or marry each other.

All the members of Umu-okudele reside in the small village of Aro with the members of five other patrilineage groups. Although they cannot trace their descent, these six patrilineages assume a common ancestry. Members of one group are permitted to marry those of another group providing there is no "exchange of blood"--as they call it. That is, once a male from one patrilineage marries a female from another patrilineage, the reverse is never allowed. Since Nwachukwu's brother married a woman from Amaohutu--another patrilineage in Aro--no male from Amaohutu can now seek to marry a female in Nwachukwu's patrilineage.

The older male members of Aro elect a chief to represent their village and to act as leader and protector of the village. The chief is a mature and respected member of the village who is elected on the basis of his ability to keep peace in the village and to be a fair and just mediator. He receives no pay for his position and can be deposed if he does not maintain fairness in handling cases.

The village of Aro along with about thirty other villages in the area make up the village-group of Uturu. There is a belief that all the villages of Uturu had one ancestor long, long ago but no one can trace this ancestry. The chiefs of the villages elect a chief of Uturu based on leadership qualities and wisdom. The chief of Uturu helps to settle conflicts between villages which most often center on land disputes.

Members of Uturu meet in a large central area (*ebe nzūko*) for festivities, e.g., wrestling, New Yam Festival, etc. Occasionally settlement of cases between villages takes place in this area under the direction of the chief of Uturu.

NETWORK OF SOCIAL RELATIONSHIPS

Among the Owerri Igbo, social groups are defined by kin and non-kin relationships. The social roles and status positions differ for each group as do the interpersonal roles. The following is a discussion of kin based social groups and their social roles; and interpersonal roles within both social groups.

<u>Kin Based Relationships</u>

Kinship defines the following sub-groups: (1) relatives by descent: nuclear family (families), compound (*èzi*), patrilineage (*ųmù nnà*), and ancestors (*nnànnà* or *ndi ichie*); and (2) relatives by marriage: in-laws (*ogò*). Members of each sub-group have certain duties and obligations towards other members of the group. The status positions of various members of the group define the societal and interpersonal roles which are supposed to exist in each group. These are discussed in detail below.

Social Roles of Patrilineage Members

Patrilineage members are supposed to exhibit a high degree of internal cohesion. The ideal behavior expected among patrilineage members is <u>brotherliness</u> which includes mutual trust, loyalty, and affection. This is reflected in the Igbo term by which they address one another, *nwa nnē m* which means 'my sibling'. It is the duty and social obligation of each lineage member to help other lineage members when possible; consult each other for advice; obey the lineage head, elder male members, and head, compound head, or nuclear family head so that a settlement can be reached immediately rather than keep conflicts hidden. Keeping conflicts between the parties involved hidden from lineage members is frowned upon and viewed as very serious, especially at the lineage level. Therefore, lineage members are constantly reporting offenses committed by fellow lineage members and often coming together for mediation.

The following proverb reflects the prescribed custom or law of the land (*omenàla*) regarding treatment of one's lineage members: *A nāghị èke ikē n'ụlọ̀*. L.T. One should not exercise power among one's kin. In effect, this proverb alludes to the principle that you are not supposed to treat your lineage members as you would treat others. When offended by fellow lineage members, one is supposed to forgive and forget as opposed to striking back or revenging. Revenge is supposed to be reserved for non-kin. Among lineage members, forgiveness is regarded as noble and the ideal; whereas among others it is regarded as a weakness and a defect. The ideal of fighting back when offended to maintain your dignity and self-respect in the community applies to non-lineage members, not lineage members.

The Owerri Igbo recognize two different types of offenses: (1) breach of taboos (*nsọ*) which refers to an offense against the earth deity and is believed to bring the anger of the ancestors who punish the lineage members or village community; and (2) breach of the laws of the land. Violation of taboos include such things as incest, homicide, and marriage with lineage members. These offenses are penally sanctioned and require certain rituals to be carried out to satisfy the offended earth (*àlà*). The second class of offenses has no supernatural reference but may vary for lineage members as opposed to non-lineage members. The gravity of the second class of offenses is determined by the social relationship between the parties involved. (See Table III).

In line with the focus on unity and solidarity of lineage members, such things as either accusing a fellow lineage member of certain crimes or "ruining their good names" (*imebī āhā mmadụ́*) in front of non-lineage members are regarded as extremely serious offenses--almost to the point of abominations (*arụ̄*).[9] They are regarded as equal to stealing or causing the death of a lineage member. Lineage members are supposed to defend fellow lineage members to outsiders at all costs whether their fellow lineage members are guilty or not. Ruining a fellow lineage member's reputation is damaging to the lineage itself as well as betraying of the strict rule of solidarity and protection which the lineage strives to maintain. Such an offense can bring an interpersonal relationship of enmity between lineage members. When this happens, the offended lineage member is not supposed to seek revenge but merely cease the duties he would normally perform for the offending lineage member. For example, the offended lineage member may cease giving or seeking advice from the offending member or he may cease visiting him or helping him when he is in need of help.

Social roles of individual patrilineage members are defined by the sub-group in the kinship hierarchy. Leadership and authority in the patrilineage are based on the fundamental ascribed characteristic of age, patrilineal descent, and sex. The head of the nuclear family (families) is the husband or the eldest living son; the head of the compound is the eldest living male in the compound; and the head of the patrilineage--the holder of ọ̀fọ--is the eldest living male in the patrilineage. The duties of each head to their respective group include:

(1) maintaining peaceful coexistence among members of the group, which includes stopping quarrels and preventing and mediating conflicts;

(2) giving advice to members of the group to keep them out of trouble or help them solve problems;

(3) supporting and protecting members from outside groups by offering sacrifices or displaying physical or intellectual superiority; and

(4) representing members whenever they are in trouble.

The members of each group in turn are obligated to seek help and advice from the head of their group when in trouble, respect him, obey him, and consult with him about any major undertaking in their life, such as marriage. Thus, the father (or eldest son, if the father is dead) is supposed to mediate conflicts among his wives and/or children; the head of the compound settles conflicts between compound members, including wives of the same husband if the husband is unsuccessful; and the lineage head settles conflicts between any lineage members and even among members of the same compound if the compound head is unsuccessful. (Table II depicts the role of mediator.)

The lineage is supported by the supernatural sanction of ọ̀fọ and it is the lineage head's major duty to see that customs or the laws of the land (omenàlà) are followed. The social sub-groups of the patrilineage are linked to each other by the leaders or heads of each group. The nuclear family head is the link between his group and the compound; the compound head is the link between his group and the lineage and the ancestors, who are the highest and ultimate enforcers of omenàlà. The most authoritative members of society are the ancestors who, although not living, symbolize the authority of the lineage.

Table II: Mediators

	Potential Mediators (defined by societal roles)	Disputants
Kin based	Fathers of husband & wife Head of the compound Father Head of the lineage Father and/or mother Husband	Husband and wife Compound members Children of same father Lineage members Children of same mother Wives of same husband
Non-kin based	Fathers Chief or councillor Town chief Husbands or elderly women Headmaster Teacher High ranking official	Children (unrelated) Village members Village-group members Married women Teachers School children Workers

Ancestors occupy a special place in Igbo religious practice. The Igbo conceive of their ancestors as the invisible segment of the lineage. . . There is a loving reverence for the deceased ancestors who are expected to come back to reincarnate and 'do to the living members what they did for them'. . . the ancestors protect the living from the wicked spirits. (Uchendu, 1965:102)

Within the nuclear family (families), the wife (wives) and children owe complete obedience to the head. In turn, the head is expected to provide for them, protect them, and advise them. When a conflict arises between co-wives or siblings, the nuclear family head is expected to settle it.

Siblings or children of the same father (umụ di) are supposed to treat each other as comrades and co-operate with each other. The senior (eldest) sibling of the nuclear family (families) has authority over his siblings. This authority includes advising them, keeping them out of trouble, disciplining them, and defending them against outsiders. His siblings are, in turn, supposed to obey and respect him. Since siblings of different mother (umụ nnē) with the same father often grow up together, they often regard each other as brothers and sisters, despite the fact that they have different mothers. However, their priorities and degree of confidence may be slightly stronger towards the siblings born of their own mother. Co-wives have the authority to settle squabbles among the children of their husband, whether they involve their very own children or not.[10] If they are unsuccessful, their husband often steps in to settle the conflict.

The ancestors of the patrilineage are a crucial part of social roles also. They hold ultimate power and authority in the society and act as enforcers of omenàlà. They are obligated to reincarnate in a physical form acceptable to the children of lineage members; to protect lineage members from being harmed by bad spirits; to enforce the laws of the land as well as ensure lineage unity by punishing through sickness, death, or human infertility lineage members who violate omenàlà; and to ensure the maintenance of tradition. In turn, living members of the lineage are obligated to follow the laws of the land (omenàlà); remember the ancestors by offering food and drink to them before partaking of any for themselves; invoke the names of ancestors during sacrifices so that the ancestors will protect them from bad spirit; and thank them for protecting the lineage members from harm. Thus, the ancestors play a very important role in Igbo society. They are believed to be the enforcers of omenàlà. They protect the living members of the patrilineage as long as omenàlà are followed, but grow angry and punish lineage members when omenàlà are no followed. As one respondent noted in reference to following certain customs regarding the marrying process: "If you fail to do the right thing, then something wrong may crop up later, because you have gone against the law of the land." This folk comment reflects a very significant belief which affects the behavior of members of Igbo culture; that is, those things not done according to omenàlà do not work out well. For example, in the case cited by the respondent if one does not follow the customs laid down by tradition when he is marrying a girl, the marriage will not work out. More generally, this belief refers to the power of the ancestors, who "know everything you do," and thus enforce omenàlà.

Social Roles of In-Laws

All females in Owerri Igbo society are supposed to marry and bear children. Because of rules of exogamy they are not permitted to marry members of their own patrilineage and in some communities they are not permitted to marry members of their own natal village (village exogamy).[11] In all cases, females must leave their own lineage group to join the lineage group of their husband. Technically, they also remain members of their original patrilineage and are free to return to their home if treated unfairly by their husband or not well-protected by him. In many cases, members of the wife's own lineage intervene in her behalf.

It is obvious that lineage exogamy or village exogamy among the Owerri Igbo functions to extend the bonds of social relationships from linage to lineage and village to village. In small villages, this can often mean that everyone is related to everyone else to some degree. Since marriage is regarded as an alliance between two sets of relatives or two villages, intervillage tensions are often softened as a result. Married females play a significant role in resolving and perhaps preventing intervillage and/or interlineage disputes.

Through marriage, the husband and his patrilineage become in-laws *(ọgọ̀)* to the patrilineage of his wife. The former group is referred to as "small in-laws" *ọgọ̀ ntā)* and the latter group is referred to as "big in-laws" *(ọgọ̀ ukwū)*. Because it is considered an act of benevolence for one lineage to give its daughter in marriage to another lineage, the husband and his lineage group *(ọgọ ntā)* are expected to treat their big in-laws) with honor and respect. They are supposed to avoid conflicts and case-making with the "big in-laws." The husband is supposed to be very careful not to do anything which would appear insulting to his "big in-laws." In particular, when visiting in the home of the "big in-laws," he is not supposed to be boastful or display any power or high status he might have. He is rather supposed to be humble and willing to assist in even the smallest of tasks. Even if insulted by a member of the wife's patrilineage ("the big in-laws"), the husband is supposed to treat such an insult very lightly or remain quiet. Conflict is avoided at all costs. An Igbo proverb refers to the expected behavior of the husband in the home of his "big in-laws": *Nwatà àmàrà ùka, ọ̀ bụghī n'obi ọgọ̀ ya*. L.T. A child shouldn't portray his wisdom of speech in his in-law's home.

In turn, the "big in-laws" are obligated to accept the "small in-laws." They are supposed to protect the wife's husband and help him out whenever possible.

Non-kin Based Roles

This discussion refers only to *diàlà* (free-born). Where kin-based roles are based on ascribed characteristics, non-kin roles are based on both ascribed and achieved characteristics, including: age, sex, ancestry *(ikwù)*, education and "intelligence."

The village is both a political and social unit. Each village regards itself as a close social unit and seeks to maintain some degree of unity and solidarity among its members. The leader of the village is usually a chief *(ezè)* who is selected democratically by elder village males according to the following achieved characteristics: wisdom or "intelligence"; knowledge of traditions and customs as well as past events in the village; ability to speak well and use proverbs; and ability to settle disputes. The chief must be male, of free-born ancestry, and is often an elder member of the village community. Some of the chief's major obligations include: giving advice; protecting the village members; representing the village to outsiders--especially the village-group; settling inter-village disputes; and maintaining peace, order, co-operation, and unity among village members.

The chief regularly is called on to mediate conflicts which do not get resolved at various levels in the kinship hierarchy. He normally handles two types of mediation: (1) personal advice and (2) summons *(itū ikpè)*. The first type is the least drastic and includes giving personal advice to one or both parties involved as a result of a complaint made to him by an offended party. He may go directly to the accused and advise him or he may call both parties together in his home and advise each one as to how to correct their error or what to do. His major goal is to make peace between the two parties which amounts to effecting reconciliation.

The second type of mediation which a village chief carries out is more serious. One party wishes to take action against an opposing party in the form of a summons. For this type of mediation, the chief is assisted by a jury which usually consists of two male representatives selected by each lineage group in the village. The offended person must pay a predetermined fee to have the accused summoned and both parties must supply food and drink for the jury, chief, and all others involved. The mediation takes place in the chief's house. After hearing each party's version of the case, cross-examining them, and calling forth witnesses and cross-examining them, the chief and his jury retire for deliberation ($igb\bar{a}$ $\dot{i}z\grave{u}$) to decide which party is right and which party is wrong as well as any compensation which one party owes to another. After deliberation, a spokesman, chosen for his power of oratory and his persuasive talents, announces the decision. If either party is dissatisfied or not persuaded by the decision reached by the chief and his jury, they may take the matter to Magistrate Court. The Magistrate Court is not a traditional means of settlement, since it was founded by the British during colonialization. Taking a matter to the Magistrate Court is regarded as a very serious step which is often disastrous to one or both parties in the dispute since the corruption of the Court causes extreme financial expense in bribes to achieve a victory.

The village-group, the widest political community, is also a social unit with a lesser degree of solidarity and unity than the village. The village-group has a chief who is selected by the leaders of the villages who make up the village-group. He is often selected according to the same qualities as that of a village chief. One of the major duties of the village-group chief is to settle disputes between villages as a whole and/or between individual members from different villages. He most commonly settles disputes involving land, debts, or bride payments. Like the village chief, anyone who has a grievance is free to request his help in settlement. Because of the desire to settle matters at the kindship level, the village-group chief most often settles matters between parties who do not share kin ties. However, if a settlement can not be reached at the kinship level or by the village chief, he may occasionally be requested to settle disputes among members of the same kin group. The village-group chief is assisted by a jury to handle disputes. Most of the disputes involving juries are over land rights. There are a variety of different ways juries are selected among the Owerri Igbo. One of the most common ways is for each village to select one or two male representatives for the particular dispute at hand. As is the case at the village level, if either of the two parties (disputants) is not satisfied with the decision reached by the chief and his jury they can take the matter to the Magistrate Court.

Members of the village and village-groups form organizations which can be referred to as "associations." They are formed on a basis

other than kinship--most often formed by agreement or contract
(Uchendu, 1965: 76). Among the Owerri Igbo the types of associations, their structure, and the way in which they interrelate may
vary from one village-group to another. Some communities among the
Owerri Igbo may have some of the following associations: age sets,
secret societies, and title societies.[12] The village-group of Uturu
from which many of the respondents for this research originate most
commonly have the following associations: work groups, women's dance
troups, and men's dance groups.[13] Although the structure and types
of associations may differ from place to place among the Owerri Igbo,
their function in terms of settling conflicts is the same. Each
association elects a leader who has the authority to settle conflicts
between members of the group.

Women among the Owerri Igbo frequently organize informally into dance
groups at the village level. Such a group holds meetings to practice dancing and singing, collects a common fund to assist members
of their group, and dresses alike when singing and dancing as a group
for different festive occasions. They elect a leader who can be
called on to settle conflicts between the members of the association.

Females have little to say in the administrative or political affairs
of the village or village-group and have no rights to land or leadership in ritual activities. However, dance groups are one vehicle
through which they can, as a group, express their disapproval and
secure their demands in the community. They are permitted to do
this through song and dance during festive occasions where the male
leaders of the village or village-group are present. Therefore,
women's dance group activities are one means through which the males
in the village are informed of the grievances of the females, and
thus these activities may function as a means of social control.

Respected people of old age are referred to as elders. Although the
elders do not necessarily form any organized group, they are worthy
of mention here because of the high status position which they occupy
by virtue of their old age and the social roles to which they are
expected to adhere. <u>Elder</u> refers to either males or females, although male elders command higher status and greater respect than
females.

In Igbo society old age is supposed to automatically confer honor
and elicit respect thereby increasing responsibility, leadership
among kin groups and the village, and wisdom, especially for males.
Male elders are expected to ensure the maintenance of tradition,
settle conflicts or disputes, warn others who are in danger, be
skillful in the use of proverbs, and be doers of good deeds. Those
who are not elders owe elders respect, obedience, trust and reverence. Because of their old age, elders are generally identified
with the ancestors--guardians and enforcers of the customs (omenàlà).
In a sense, the elders are regarded as the living ancestors and
therefore their authority is backed by supernatural support. In
addition, old age is held in very high respect among the Owerri Igbo
because it is believed that those who obey the laws of the land
(omenàlà) live to an old age.

INTERPERSONAL RELATIONSHIPS: FRIEND AND ENEMY

For the Owerri Igbo, interpersonal roles among non-kin groups differ from interpersonal roles among kin groups. Two interpersonal roles are mentioned for this research: friend and enemy. These roles for kin based groups have been discussed previously. This section only discusses interpersonal roles among non-kin based groups.

Because age-mates tend to associate more with each other, friends are most commonly age-mates. However, age is not necessarily a restriction or the basis of friendship. Those in different age groups quite often become friends because of the reciprocation of good deeds toward one another. Friendship is restricted to members of the same sex necessarily.

Among non-kin based groups, the Owerri Ogbo folk conception of friendship is: helping and doing good deeds for another or a member of one's own kin group. Friends are obligated to: (1) represent each other well to others; (2) wish each other good; (3) warn one another of danger; (4) defend each other when in trouble; and (5) help each other to progress or advance in any way possible.[14] The folk conception of enmity is: offending or causing harm to another or a member of another person's kin group. Enemies are expected to: (1) misrepresent each other to others which includes telling lies about each other behind the other person's back to lower his reputation in the eyes of the community; (2) wish each other evil; (3) not warn each other of danger and in fact often plan ways in which the other person can be harmed or put into danger; (4) delight in each other's misfortunte or that of members of the other person's kin group; and (5) try to prevent each other from progessing or advancing in any way possible.

Regarding both the role of friend and enemy, there is a keen awareness among the Owerri Igbo that individuals from different kin groups can easily move from the role of friend to that of enemy at any time and once the enemy role begins it is next to impossible for those individuals to return to the role of friend, since forgetting and forgiveness among non-kin members is not expected. In addition, it appears that enmity is easily established since those who begin to feel you are not for them or in agreement with them, consider you to be against them and their enemy. In Igbo culture, those who do not have sufficient diplomatic skill in speaking and dealing with others to enable them to remain neutral often have many enemies. Because of the easily established role of enemy, as well as the dreadful outcomes of enmity (discussed below), "intelligent" members of Igbo culture are cautious in their treatment of others and careful not to reveal or share certain types of information with those outside of their kin group, for this information may later be used against them when the enemy role is assumed.

The prescribed cultural principle is to avoid offending or hurting others. Once one is offended, he is expected to point out the offense to the offender, but if the offender does not show regret or does not discontinue his offense the prescribed reaction is to fight back and seek revenge. Those members of the community who do not affirm their ability to defend themselves by fighting back are considered weaklings by the members of the community and soon others come to take what they can from them and begin to push them around. More survival becomes fairly difficult as a result. It is through the display of strength towards one's enemy that the individual maintains his dignity, respect, and rights in the society. Inability to display strength results in loss of these. Strength (*ikè*) includes both physical and intellectual prowess. Both are highly respected among the Owerri Igbo as revealed through wrestling matches in which all males participate at some point in their life as a test of both strength and intelligence. Those who are victorious in these matches gain respect in the community and are usually free from ridicule or insults from others because others fear their strength. This explains why threats by powerful individuals are so effective in getting others to change their ways.

Between enemies, "intelligence" refers primarily to being able to attack and hurt the opponent without in turn getting hurt. This usually includes shrewd and cunning acts which involve utilizing any information regarding the opponent considered shameful by the members of the society, e.g., demeaning acts, breaches of custom, debt, etc. The enemy role requires using detrimental information against the opponent in <u>public</u>; that is, outside of the kinship circle. This normally comes about either through an exchange of words (*iliā olilia*) or gossiping (*igbā àsìrì*). The goal is to ruin or damage the opponent's reputation in the community. Friends avoid sharing confidential information which could be regarded as disgraceful with other friends from other kin groups, for if ever they become enemies they pay a heavy price. An Igbo proverb sums this up very well: *Ųkà a kàrà àkà mà adì mmà, mà adī n̄jō à kpàa isī*. L.T. What you tell someone when you are friends changes when conflict comes in.

FOLK CONCEPTIONS

To understand social relations more clearly and their connection to conflict, it is important to understand two broad folk conceptions among the Owerri Igbo. Custom or the "law of the land" (*omenàlà*) and "intelligence" (*àmàmihe*). These are conceived by the Owerri Igbo as being closely interrelated to each other. They are both fundamental to the understanding of conflict (*èsèmokwu*) in Igbo society.

The Law of the Land (*omenàlà*)

Omenàlà is an extremely important principle among the Owerri Igbo. It is in fact the main foundation on which the actions of the Owerri Igbo rest. *Omenàlà* are the prescribed mores set down by tradition. They specify the ideal behavior according to tradition. In particular, they specify how other members in the society are to be treated, which is manifested in social, interpersonal, and interactional roles. Because the land is regarded as not only sacred but also the home of the ancestors, omenàlà. really constitute the sacred customary laws of the Owerri Igbo. There is a strong belief among the Owerri Igbo that if these sacred laws are followed, there is peace or social order. However, if they are not followed there is conflict or disorder because the ancestors have been annoyed. The ancestors are believed to hold tremendous power and authority over the lives of living lineage members. As one Igbo respondent put it: "If the land (àlà) is annoyed with you, you may not live up to three hours." Thus the emphasis among the Owerri Igbo--at least in traditional society--is on following the omenàlà.

A great many proverbs make reference to some of these omenàlà. This is one reason these proverbs are so commonly used in conflict situations, particularly in mediation. Also, because many proverbs make reference to these sacred laws (omenàlà), they are highly regarded and carry a great deal of prestige among the Owerri Igbo.

It's important to note that the notion of "intelligence" among the Owerri Igbo is very different from that found in many societies in the Western world. It is firmly grounded in the basic principles of the culture itself and generally refers to qualities required to survive and also advance one's status position in Igbo culture. "Intelligence" is an achieved characteristic which confers more prestige among the Owerri Igbo than other achieved characteristics such as formal education, wealth, or physical strength. It is believed that once one has "intelligence" he can easily achieve any of these characteristics as well as be a successful leader in the community. A folk definition offered by one Igbo respondent for "intelligence" was: "Being able to handle matters on the spur of the moment in a nice way . . . one who can prevent something bad from happening, but if something bad heppens he can suggest constructive measures to check it."

The folk conception of "intelligence" held by the Owerri Igbo can be described under two broad frameworks: (1) knowing and applying the laws of the land; and (2) using the appropriate strategies to achieve one's goal.

Knowing and Applying the Law of the Land

Those adults who do not know and apply omenàlà are regarded as unintelligent or stupid. For children, this lack of knowledge and skill might be forgiven and expected, but for adults it is not. Those who are the oldest members of the community--the elders--are expected to possess this knowledge of omenàlà to a greater degree than younger members of the community. The ability to use proverbs reflects skill and possession of this knowledge. In fact, in the words of one Igbo respondent: "If you don't use proverbs, people will think you are not mature, you are just a child." This is so because, "The common language any fool can go about it, but the use of proverbs displays your intelligence and maturity in that language and experience."

When older members of the society perform actions which do not conform to the omenàlà, they can be and are often reprimanded by younger male members of the society or laughed at by their fellow elders. In relationship to this aspect of the notion of "intelligence" held by the Owerri Igbo, it is also expected that one who has "intelligence" knows how to react or what to do when *omenàlà* are transgressed. When one transgresses certain customary laws there are certain rituals and other actions which must be carried out by the appropriate member of the society to rectify the violation of *omenàlà*.

"Knowing and applying the laws of the land" also refers to playing one's societal, interpersonal, or interactional role successfully. Those who are more skillful in following the ideal patterns of behavior or specific roles are considered more "intelligent."

Craftiness *(aghụghọ)*

Adaptability is a key aspect of "intelligence"--according to the folk conception. Those who never vary their pattern of behavior with changing circumstances have difficulty in achieving their goals among the Owerri Igbo and are therefore not regarded as "intelligent." To achieve one's goals--which most often include status advancement through acquisition of wealth and leadership--an "intelligent" member of Owerri Igbo society deals with other members of his society successfully. This most often means that he is able to choose the most appropriate and unexpected type of behavior. "Intelligence" in this sense refers to craftiness (*aghụghọ*). For example, when attempting revenge, an intelligent person utilizes the appropriate strategies to achieve his goal of hurting his opponent yet he avoids being hurt in turn. When speaking with others, an "intelligent" person is able to obtain confidential information (weaknesses or defects) about other non-kin group members without revealing weaknesses or defects about himself or his kin group members.

In Igbo society leaders of non-kin groups are democratically elected according to the consensus of the other members of the group. Because of this, those who obtain leadership positions are considered "intelligent" because they are very skillful in dealing with others. Above all, they are skilled in the art of diplomacy, and they are capable of maintaining a certain type of neutrality when speaking with others so that they do not alienate others. They are able to win others over, even when the views and ways of various groups are very much in conflict. Above all, they are able to speak in a very diplomatic way which helps them avoid turning others against them or making enemies. According to a comment by one Igbo respondent: "Intelligence is often dictated by the way you speak and the way you give speeches." Those who speak diplomatically often are very general and non-specific as well as non-commital in any extreme direction. All of these qualities enable one to unite groups among the Owerri Igbo and thus obtain leadership positions. In fact, those most skillful in the use of proverbs often gain leadership positions as pointed out in the statement by one Igbo respondent:

> People can be elected to be sent out to speak to other groups if they can use proverbs well, because the group knows he wouldn't get them into trouble; the person able to use proverbs to escape from being cornered by others.

SEMIOTICS OF CONFLICT

Conflicts in the Igbo society of southeastern Nigeria, and perhaps other African societies as well, provide important information regarding patterns of interaction as well as the use of language.[15] Conflict is viewed by members of traditional Igbo society as an upset in personal and social relations which, if not prevented or stopped, can develop into gradually more serious stages. The Igbo term èsèmokwu, literally the "dragging of words," refers to "a disagreement that is going to result in case-making."[16] Conflicts can develop in a variety of elaborate ways and at each state in the development, there are prescribed ways of conflict management handed down for ages and ages by tradition. In all cases these traditional ways involve communicative strategies which are crucial to a successful prevention, reduction, or resolution of the conflict. Proverbs and other types of quotes are necessary verbal tools which are used to achieve the primary goal of conflict reduction.

There are two possible reasons for the traditional emphasis on conflict reduction. The first is that many conflicts arise from a breach of omenàlà--the prescribed mores and customs left by tradition which specify the obligations and rights of members of the society toward one another. Since the ancestors are vested with the authority to enforce these sacred laws and customs, they hold tremendous power and authority over the lives of the living. Contravention of omenàlà can anger the ancestors to the point of punishing family members involved or the entire community. Therefore, members of the community, especially elders and/or leaders, view it their responsibility to take the necessary steps to adjust social relations among the living and hence restore peace with the ancestors. The Igbo world view as summarized by Uchendu (1965: 13), a well-known anthropologist and also a member of Igbo society, suggests:

> . . . the Igbo believe that [these] social calamities and cosmic forces which disturb their world are controllable and should be 'manipulated' by them for their own purpose. The maintenance of social and cosmological balance in the world becomes, therefore, a dominant and pervasive theme in Igbo life. . . . Indeed, whatever threatens the life of the individual or his security as well as society is interpreted by the Igbo as a sign of warning that things must be set right before they get out of hand.

Part of this world view is based on the ideal of social justice on which peaceful co-existence rests for the Igbo.[17] Only when the prescribed mores of the society are followed is social justice conceived to exist and it then results in a balance of social relationships. However, when these relationships are disturbed, social injustice prevails and can only be amended through the peaceful adjustment of the disturbed social relationships.

The second reason for the emphasis on conflict reduction is the awareness of the serious implications of conflict development in terms of financial expense as well as the disruption of social relations not only between the two parties involved, but also their relatives and other members of the community, especially if the conflict should go in the most serious direction *ikpē ìkpe*--"going to court." Nowadays, this refers to the Magistrate Court, a system originally created by the British during colonization and one which often works in contradiction to the ideal goal of conflict resolution in Igbo society. Rather than seeking to arrive at a compromise or resolution acceptable to both parties, the Magistrate Court seeks to pinpoint a "winner" and a "loser" according to British rules and regulations of law or perhaps Nigerian rules which were derived from the former. Since one side always loses, the conflict is not resolved but rather it makes permanent the ill-feeling between the opposing parties so that any attempts to restore a peaceful relation through traditional, more successful means is almost impossible.

Although the cultural ideal is to stop or reduce the development of the conflict, in reality conflicts are often furthered either as a result of an unsuccessful attempt to reduce them or as a result of a successful attempt to increase the conflict by one or both of the opposing parties. Proverbs and other types of quotes are equally useful communicative strategies in this aspect of conflict as well.

MANAGEMENT OF CONFLICT

Conflicts can potentially develop between any members of the society whatever their role or status position. Thus, opposing parties can consist of individuals, groups, or entire villages. However, at a further point in its development, the conflict is traditionally managed by those who have authority over or responsibility for involved parties. It is quite common for husbands to intervene on behalf of their wives or parents to intervene on behalf of their children. For example, if two married women end up in conflict, resolution may be reached by their husbands even if the wives are not present. Once the two husbands arrive at a settlement to the misunderstanding, they use their personal authority over their wives to see that the further development of the conflict is prevented, since their wife is expected to obey them.

In Igbo society and perhaps in many other African societies as well, there are two distinct groups: kin groups and non-kin groups. Conflicts traditionally are managed slightly differently within kin groups as opposed to outside of kin groups. Certainly, the degree of seriousness of violations of social mores (*omenàlà*) differs from one group to the other. Table III below illustrates some typical violations in order of seriousness for the two distinct groups. Whereas the offense within the kin group often only leads to a suspension of duties and/or obligations towards the offending lineage member, serious offenses committed by non-kin members often lead to revenge or "court case."[18] Because of the strong emphasis on family solidarity, more effort is applied to resolve conflicts involving lineage members and to prevent these conflicts from going further, especially from going to Magistrate Court. A court case among famil (kin) members openly displays a lack of internal cohesion of a kin group and can lead to not only public embarrassment in the community but also an invitation to non-kin members to take advantage of or pr on members of the kin group who have exposed their weakness publicly

Table III: Offenses Leading to Conflict

KIN MEMBERS	NON-KIN MEMBERS
(least)	
-ingratitude for a favor	-ingratitude for a favor
-failure to fulfill social obligations (respect to elders)	-selfishness or exploitation of another
-failure to repay debt	-breach of trust (releasing confidential information)
-insulting another	-getting unmarried or widow pregnant
-selfishness or exploitation of another	-insulting another
-claiming land ownership of another's property	-false accusations (malicious gossip)
-theft	-failure to fulfill community obligations
-breach of trust (leaking confidential information to non-kin)	-failure to repay a debt
-false accusations (malicious gossip)	-claiming ownership of another's land or property
(most)	-theft
-incest (sexual relations with kin member)	-murder of non-kin member
-murder of kin member (Taboo nso)	

Although certain violations, such as theft and false accustion, are usually sanctioned more severely in Igbo society, the cause of the conflict is not the only or even the primary determinant of the likelihood of conflict development.[19] Most crucial is the relationship between the participants involved. For example, in non-kin groups if there is a previous relationship of enmity between the two parties involved, the conflict will usually develop very differently than if there is a previous relationship of friendship. The interpersonal relationships often influence the management of conflicts between non-kin members quite extensively.

It is obvious from the preceding discussion that conflicts at any state in their development are extremely sensitive issues. Traditional Igbo society has an inbuilt means of preventing, reducing, or resolving many conflicts in a very personalized way. The success of actually managing the conflict in a positive direction often depends upon the use of traditional communicative strategies at each stage of the conflict. In fact each stage (to be discussed below) can be viewed as a specific "speech event" (Hymes 1967) with its specific goal and roles of the participants. Successful conflict managers are skilled in using proverbs and other types of quotes as a verbal strategy to manipulate one or both parties involved into changing their actions so as to conform to the prescriptive mores and values of the society. Quotes are perhaps the key to conflict management because they innately depersonalize statements which might otherwise be taken as attacks, insults, accusations. Quotes, therefore, perform a key role in actually rectifying relationships between participants in the conflict rather than inflaming these relationships. Quotes, thus, are a crucial communicative strategy in Igbo society in the management of conflicts. Illustrations of exactly how this is enacted will be described later in detail.

COMMUNICATIVE STAGES OF CONFLICT

Just as Western societies have an institutionalized system (the courts) of dealing with conflict, Igbo society has a traditional, institutionalized means of managing conflict at each stage of its development. In Igbo society conflicts are managed in "speech events" which may seem less formalized than the court system in the Western world but which nevertheless have traditional rules and regulations specified by the culture informally.

The conflict sequence is extremely complex, but for the sake of brevity we can note the most obvious points in conflict development. These points can be viewed essentially as speech events which are commonly referred to by Igbo speakers and which are generally characterized by specific participant roles. Table V below illustrates the obvious points of conflict development in terms of communication events.

Table IV depicts the specific proverbs collected in the data for each particular interactional event.

Table IV. Proverbs Quoted in Interactional Events

Interactional Event	Proverbs quoted (see Appendix C: Index)
1. idū odū (advise)	6, 16, 19, 22, 23, 26, 28, 31, 32, 35, 42, 45, 53, 56
2. mkpari (insult)	2, 11, 15, 22, 29, 33, 48, 49, 67, 70
3. imenye egsū (intimidate)	3, 12, 13, 25, 27, 36, 44, 52, 58, 59, 65
4. ikwū okwu (point out mistake)	7, 8, 9, 10, 14, 17, 20, 24, 30, 35, 39, 41, 45, 47, 51, 54, 64
5. iliā olilia (exchanging words)	2, 10, 15, 22, 47, 48, 49
6. idozī okwu (mediation)	7, 21, 34, 37, 38, 43, 50, 53, 57, 61, 68, 69
7. ikpē ikpè (general statements)	40, 66

Table V: Obvious Stages in Conflict Development

Terms for Speech Event	Folk Definition	Goal in Conflict	Participant Roles
idū odū "advise"	"you warn somebody of the consequences of his action"	prevent	advisor & advisee
mkpari "insult"	"doing things that will hurt another's feelings or degrade him"	reduce	offended & accused
imenye egwū "intimidate"	"threatening through boasting"	reduce	offended & accused
iliā olilia "exchanging words"	"a verbal duel of insults in public"	reduce	adversaries
idozī okwu "peacemaking"	"putting things in order or settling a dispute"	resolve	mediator & disputants
imebī āhā mmadù "slander"	"spoiling other people's names; negatively misrepresenting other people; malicious gossip"	increase	offended & accused
ikpē ìkpè "general statements"	"using words that refer to certain people without mentioning their names"	increase or reduce	offended
ikpē ìkpe "litigation"	"court settlement; a formal means of settling a case with a judge and disputants; it is not aimed at cooling people down but trying to bring out what will make the opponent suffer"	increase	adversary

Idū odū is advice given freely and frequently in Igbo society by those (advisors) concerned for the well-being of the other party (advisee). Unsolicited advice is commonly given as a comment about the on-going behavior of the other party or as a suggestion regarding future behavior to help the advisee avoid getting into conflict. "Wise" people are expected to be grateful for the advice and utilize it to keep them out of danger. As one Igbo speaker put it: "advice helps you know the things to do and it's supposed to help you know the line of direction or action to take."

Mkparị is an insult often used against a person ("accused") by another ("offended") who feels his own integrity has been reproached or that the accused party has tried to take advantage of him. Oddly enough, this act of retaliation often serves to reduce conflict development if the verbal strategies that are used convince the accused that the offended is equally intelligent and powerful, so that the accused will withdraw. *Mkparị* is a communicative strategy typically used when the relationship between two parties is a negative or deteriorated one. To the extent that the accused withdraws, it is successful; however, if the accused in turn retaliates at that moment the conflict can escale into *iliā ọlịlịa*.

Imenye egwū or intimidation is a communicative strategy used when the relationships of the two parties involved become even more deteriorated than in the above situation. Threats are often used as a sort of last recourse after repeated warnings have been given to the accused. Intimidations often consist of promises to restore justice through revenge or reminders that the Gods will restore this justice if the deliberate acts of aggression are not ceased. The purpose of the intimidation is obviously to frighten the accused party into stopping his actions and to the extent to which it does this, *imenye egwū* is a successful communicative strategy in managing conflict.

It is interesting that quotes, especially proverbs, are particularly useful in *imenye egwū* since they are never acceptable testimony in court for placing guilt on the user if misfortune befalls the person threatened.

Iliā ọlịlịa is an exchange of words in a bitter way in a speech event which always has an audience and often can inflame a conflict rather than reduce it.[20] *Iliā ọlịlịa* is a speech event which may develop out of the above two events (insulting or intimidating); however, it may also develop as a result of a covert conflict which eventually surfaces openly to public knowledge. This speech event is characterized by an emphasis on performance before an audience in which victory is achieved through destruction of another party's reputation either through what is said or how it is said. A defeat can come through the actual verbal exchange or through skillful use of communicative strategies, e.g., proverbs or other types of quotes.

Idozī okwu or mediation is probably the most commonly practiced speech event for managing conflicts. There are several different levels of mediation and several different terms in Igbo which explain these, but we will only discuss *idozī okwu*. *Idozī okwu* is a speech event consisting of the disputants and a mediator. In some cases only one of the disputants may be present and in other cases someone may substitute as a neutral third party in behalf of a disputant. Many mediations are planned and follow a traditional set procedure to give each disputant his fair share in narrating his case; others are spontaneous but equally have set procedures traditionally followed. The mediator's role is to maintain the peaceful coexistence of disputants in the community and more immediately to arrive at a compromise or resolution to the conflict. If chosen by the disputants, mediators are chosen because they are trusted and respected to be fair and wise or have a reputation in the community for settling disputes. In reality, a mediator is in a slightly precarious position since he must persuade both disputants to accept a resolution which may not totally be in favor of one or even both of them. It is primarily through the use of skill in communicative strategies, e.g., proverbs and other quotes, that he successfully reaches a resolution. If he is skillful in the use of quotes, he can quite often even get one disputant to accept his guilt, without losing face or marring his reputation in the community. The important point to note here is that contrary to the Magistrate Court imported from Britain, the mediator "seeks to get a compromise solution and make the two parties discontinue their dispute and make peace; the main goal is to see that both parties come back together again and become happy and enjoy each other."

Imebī āhā mmadu refers to spoiling other people's names behind their backs through gossip. It is one common communicative strategy to covert conflict development. It is a means of revenge usually when the conflict has not taken an overt type of development. Overt development may be dangerous for one of the disputants, particularly if the disputant is weaker financially or otherwise. Backbiting is one convenient means of attaining revenge and quotes are consequently a safe and handy communicative strategy to avoid being implicated if discovered since they have such multiple interpretations. The backbiter is partially covered by the form of the message he uses.

Ikpē ìkpe involves almost an entire ceremony where people are called together, sometimes in groups or even villages. One side tells their version of the story and the other side tells their version. The third person, a judge, is left to settle the matter according to court proceedings. *Ikpē ìkpe* is viewed as the ultimate means of conflict development: "if things can't be settled by *idozī okwu*, they come to this." The main goal in court settlement is to measure things according to how law has set it and whoever suffers is of little concern here. The object of this occasion of interaction is to "find out who is wrong and punish him." Obviously, compromise or even peaceful settlement is not an expected outcome of *ikpē ìkpe*.

As the Igbo terms and folk definitions briefly discussed above illustrate, Igbo society has a variety of different communicative strategies for verbally dealing with conflict development. Some of these strategies serve to reduce or resolve the conflict development, whereas in reality some may in fact increase the development of the conflict or at least maintain it. Quotes, such as proverbs, were found to be used at each stage in conflict development to maximally achieve the communicative goal of the speaker; however, other verbal means not involving quotes can also be used. A rather detailed discussion of the conflict sequence in Igbo society is provided below along with examples of the use of proverbs as a communicative strategy at crucial points in the sequence. Appendix C provides a decision-making model of potential conflict development.[21]

CONFLICT SEQUENCE

The first potential stage in the flow of interactional settings is aimed at the prevention of a conflict in an advice-giving situation; *idū odū*. In Igbo society advice is given when, as one Igbo speaker put it, "something isn't going the way it should go." Advice is viewed in Igbo society as an act of special concern for another's conflict. Proverbs are commonly used at this stage of conflict development to comment on the behavior of an advisee or make suggestions regarding future behavior so as to help him avoid getting into conflict or more trouble. For example, two people (see Adaku and Chinyelu below) are at odds and a third party may intervene with a proverb to advise one or both of the two of the dangerous direction in which they may be heading.

Case #1

> Two women, Adaku and Chinyelu were good friends. They got along very well together. One day they chatted at length happily with each other. The next day Chinyelu entered Adaku's compound. She was very angry. She began yelling "Where is Adaku? Where is Adaku?" Then she began to curse and abuse Adaku. Adaku was very surprised; she began to reply in anger. Then another woman in the compound who knew that Adaku and Chinyelu got along well together turned to Adaku and said in Chinyelu's presence: *"Onye pūtārā ụra utụtụ ọkukọ chụba yā ọsọ, ya gbàwa n'ihi na ọ māghī mà o puru ezē n'àbàlì.* L.T. Any one who wakes in the morning and is chased by a chicken should run away because he doesn't know whether the chicken developed teeth during the night. That is, Adaku should leave and not to stay and quarrel with Chinyelu because apparently there was a sudden change of feelings, which was very unusual since Chinyelu didn't act like that previously. Adaku left and Chinyelu had no recourse but to leave also. [Whether the conflict terminated here was not specified],

As in the above example, *idū odū* is used by friends to help each other but even more commonly by older or wiser relatives to help prevent the development of conflicts or problems which they most certainly would later be involved in managing.[23] For example, if an elder relative learned that a younger relative was constantly getting himself into trouble, such as school fights or other matters, he might call him aside one day and discuss this, ending up with advice in a proverb, such as: *"A gbaa àkụ ọ tụ n'ogwe, a gbaa àkụ* ọ́ tụ n'ogwe, ọ̀ bụ̀ ogwe kà a pììrì àkụ?" (L.T. An arrow is shot, it hits a log. An arrow is shot, it hits the same log. Is it this log the arrow is meant for?). This is a way of letting the younger relative know that he will be blamed even if he happens to be innocent because of his past actions, so he had better change them.

When advice is not rendered or is not effective in stopping those actions which can lead to conflict, someone feels that an unjust act or an offense has been committed against him. He then begins to play the role of an "offended" person. There are then three typical ways the conflict can turn at this point and all three depend upon how the offended chooses to respond to the offense. He may react in an open manner by merely pointing out the offense to the accused or he may contact a third party for mediation or he may plan to revenge at a later more opportune moment. Each of these responses are dealt with in more detail below.

Pointing out an offense may simply be a matter of calling the accused party to order in a fairly positive, unangry way. Proverbs are commonly used in these cases when the accused is of higher status or power than the offended party and a bit of caution must be exercised as the following example of workers who feel offended or mistreated by their boss.

Case #2

Several men were working for the same boss. They all expected to be treated equally; however, their boss began showing partiality by treating a few of them better than the others. Those who felt they were not being treated fairly and equally came to the boss and expressed their complaint adding that, "Ehi sī mèe ya kà e mèrè ibè ya kamà a hūnā yā n'ọkụ." (L.T. The cow says you can do anything to me but don't roast me on the fire like you do other animals).

Two other common means of point out an offense are slightly more inflamed and less cautious: *mkpari* and *imenye egwū*. Quotes are used in both cases by skillful verbal speakers and are even more powerful than ordinary language. Insults (*mkpari*) are perhaps one step removed from intimidation. *Mkpari* usually occurs when the offended is fairly certain that the accused purposely offended as the example of the two ladies below illustrates.

Case #3

Two women, Nwafọ and Mgbokwo, were neighbors. They were not, however, close friends but rather casual friends. One day Nwafọ ran out of palm oil for cooking and came to borrow some from Mgbokwo. Mgbokwo told her to go and take some from the shelf. Nwafọ took the bottle of palm oil but instead of taking only the small amount needed for cooking, she almost used all the oil and returned the bottle to Mgbokwo. When Mgbokwo saw that Nwafọ had taken more than she needed for cooking, and had not only been greedy but had also tried to take advantage of her kindness, Mgbokwo told Nwafọ, "I kwē onye ikpèchì naka ibì ọmà àgụwa yā." (L.T. If you shake hands with someone who has yaws, he will soon want to embrace you). Then Nwafọ realized that Mgbokwo was annoyed because Nwafo's actions suggested that she was taking advantage of Mgbokwo. [It was not stated whether the conflict continued later or was resolved at that point].

Imenye egwū or intimidation is offered when the offended has no doubt repeatedly warned the accused to stop his action but he apparently does not heed to this warning. A threat is a sort of last resort. A schoolteacher uses a proverb below to not only threaten his students but more or less forewarn of an action he later took.

Case #4

Mr. Eke was a school teacher. One day his class was very noisy. He tried so many techniques to quiet the class but they continued disobeying him and making noise. Several times he begged them to be quiet but they would not do so. Finally, in anger he told them, "*Nnụ̀nụ̀ fèe ajọ̄ ūfē, à gbànyèrè ya ājọ̄ ākụ̄.*" (L.T. A swift bird requires a swift bow to catch it). That is, he had been telling them to be quiet and they had refused. Now he would treat them accordingly. The next day the teacher gave the class a compulsory examination. Those who failed were forced to repeat the entire course again.

There are two possible traits that make proverbs useful tools in intimidation. In terms of effect, they provide the maximum power to a threat, since they are linked with the ancestors who command authority in Igbo society and are the ultimate enforcers of *omenàlà*. This quality makes it difficult to oppose and even harder to counter, since the only acceptable equivalent counter-comment is another suitable proverb. In addition, the general and indirect nature of the proverb makes it a powerful tool of intimidation because no details are specified as to when, where, or how revenge will be carried out. Since the accused is left with only a promise of misfortune, but no details which would enable him to ward off or fight the misfortune, the potential fear is increased. At the same time, the proverb serves as a protective device for the offended. It protects him from repercussions he might suffer at a later date as a result of his threats. Accusations and threats are serious matters in Igbo society, and there are strong penalties in the society for their use In addition, accusations or threats can serve as evidence in trials to determine guilt. If misfortune befalls a person who has been threatened, he can hold the threatener accountable and take him to court where his words may be used as strong evidence to convict him. Although acceptable testimony usually consists of exact words, the exact words of proverbs are rarely considered acceptable evidence since the objects and ideas to which they refer are far removed from their implication. Also, their ambiguous nature makes their specific meanings difficult to interpret without knowledge of all of the interactional factors. In any case, in Igbo society anyone who tries to build a case based on the implications of proverbs or who tries to hold another responsible for insult based on the use of proverbs is ridiculed and laughed at by the members of the societ Therefore, offended people who have a skillful knowledge of proverb can use quotes to protect themselves as well as effectively intimidate the accused into ceasing their actions.

As mentioned previously, a second alternative of an "offended" person may include contacting a third party for mediation. Actually, this response can potentially occur at any other point in the conflict sequence whether at an initial stage or a fairly developed stage, although the most hopeful outcome occurs at an initial stage of the conflict before too many other relatives or other parties get involved. Mediation or *idozī okwu* is a common occurrence in Igbo society and often an effective means of resolving conflicts. Quotes are very crucial in *idozī okwu* will be explained later in greater detail. Mediations, however, may be spontaneous or planned, with only one disputant there or with both disputants and/or others.[24]

During mediation the offended tries to persuade the mediator of the validity of his own version of the story as does the accused, once the mediator approaches him. Ultimately, the mediator usually must make a judgment as to who has committed an offense and as to atonement procedures to be followed. Depending upon the similarity and the evidence cited in the two versions of the story, the mediator may be able to decide in one party's favor after hearing each side of the story or he may find it necessary to bring both disputants together and have them each recount their story to him during a planned mediation where he would have more opportunity to examine each disputant further for the "truth." The mediator's objective is to peacefully resolve the conflict, but he is successful in doing so only to the extent that his judgment or management of the *idozī okwu* is accepted by both parties. Below is an example of *idozī okwu* and quotes used to resolve a dispute.

Case #5

> Two male friends, Obinna and Okafo, got into a disagreement because Obinna had told another person a secret entrusted to him by Okafo. Both Obinna and Okafo went to a neutral person (a mediator) who attempted to restore their friendship. After hearing Obinna's version of the story and Okafo's version of the story, the mediator decided that Obinna had committed a breach of trust. He then told Obinna, "*Kà ahā èri, anāghī èri ibe ha.*" (L.T. The group that eats together doesn't eat each other). That is, he had attempted to break a golden rule. Obinna felt ashamed that he had been discovered and he felt guilty. Realizing the wisdom in what the mediator had said, he refrained from breaking the trust of Okafo in the future.

When mediation is attempted after an "exchange of words," *ilịa ọlịlịa,* it is spontaneous and the mediator is usually self-chosen. In other instances, as the case above, mediation is a planned event and the mediator is chosen by the disputants who feel he is mature, just, and skilled in the traditional ways of Igbo culture. In highly planned events, often other members of the society who are involved as a result of social ties or relationship participate in the mediation making it a more formal procedure. At the end of the entire procedure, the mediator must make a decision in which he in essence skillfully convinces all those involved of the justness of his decision. His statements may involve: (1) advice to both parties; (2) a verdict pointing out the mistake to one or both parties; or (3) a justification of his verdict. For example, in a dispute between kin members who refuse to listen to their leader and take his advice, the mediator may advise: *"Ugo ọkụkọ nwère bụ abubā ya."* (L.T. The dignity of a fowl is its feathers.). This would be to let the kin members realize that there is a person who stands as the pillar of the family or group and he should be respected.

A mediator might use the following quote to justify his verdict of guilty against one of the disputants: *"Onye ejedoro n'ụkwụ ose, ghoro ose."* (L.T. A person caught in a pepper garden is accused of stealing peppers). This is to say that even if the disputant was innocent of the deed for which he may be accused, the fact that he was circumstantially there where he didn't belong demands a guilty verdict. By justifying his verdict with a quote, the mediator cleverly avoids getting blamed himself and also gives the blamed disputant a chance to "save his face" slightly. In short, it is obvious that mediators often have a higher status than disputants and are commonly leaders of the social group of the disputants. They, therefore, often use the authority derived from this status along with their leadership to pressure disputants using skillful communicative strategies into a settlement.

A third response which an offended person may make to an offense is to plan revenge at a later more opportune moment. Nursing a grudge the offended party can carry out justice himself through an act of revenge, either overtly or covertly. Nursing a grudge is the most covert form of conflict development and it is also the most serious threat to peaceful co-existence in the society, since the ill-feeling is not made known to other members of the society and consequently there is then no attempt to reduce or resolve a continuing conflict. The covert alternative to the development of the conflict is also more serious because such actions, according to Uchendu (1965: 14), are viewed as evil in Igbo society:

> Secretive persons who 'bury injuries in their minds' are held in contempt, they are often the victims of unwarranted aggression and targets of sorcery accusations. They hinder social adjustment through human interdependence.

The covert alternative, which consists primarily of attempts to carry out revenge against the opposing party, can be carried out in a variety of different ways which are quite complex, including trying to convince other individuals not to help the accused in any way or persuading other individuals who may have financial capability to sue the accused party in court. One communicative strategy quite effective in covert conflict is *imebī ahụ mmadụ,* "backbiting or slander." Quotes are used quite often to ruin the accused party's reputation by misrepresenting their name. As one Igbo speaker put it: "the person may be good but because of the picture you paint of him no one will like to call him a good name." For

Ethnography of Quoting Behavior   59

example, if two people are discussing the newly acquired material goods of another and wondering just where this person obtained the money to buy these things, an offended party might attain some bit of revenge by adding that they were supposedly acquired with money from a rich uncle and then add the quote: "*Nwanyi jì ukwu ya gata ihe, ha sì nà ụmụ di ya nyère ya.*" (L.T. When a woman gets gifts by prostitution, she says her husband's relatives gave them to her). Such a quote would be an effective way of revenging by slandering the name of the accused who is not present to suggest that when a person gets something illicitly, they tend to give preposterous explanations to support how they got them.

Reputation is a vital factor in the group-oriented society of the Igbos where everyone's actions are everybody's business. Unlike many Western societies, actions are performed in Igbo society in regard to community conscience rather than individual conscience. An individual's reputation exists under the watchful eyes of the community members. Therefore, destruction of one's reputation or character is very damaging because it snipes at the very identity of the individual and makes survival in a community, where interdependence is the theme, very difficult (Uchendu, 1965). The most dreaded happening is to have one's reputation damaged, because the results of this are felt by the individual from all directions.

Reputation is earned basically in two different ways in Igbo society: (1) in <u>public</u> during planned interactional events where speech-making predominates, or at unplanned interactional events such as an exchange of words or other occasions of interaction typically found in bars or get-togethers; and (2) in <u>private</u> through gossip during which other members of the community are freely discussed, criticized, or praised. The adversary role can attempt to tarnish the reputation or character of the opposing adversary verbally in public or in private. The adversary who is most successful in destroying the other's character, without in turn being destroyed, is the victor.

A less stinging way to achieve revenge in covert conflict is through "general statements" or *ikpē ìkpè*. These are statements made in public usually through speech making to attack an opponent who is often present. The attack is indirect and general yet public; consequently, it is quite painful many times even if the audience may not understand the true rationale behind it. The following example illustrates *ikpē ìkpè* with the use of a proverb to degrade an opponent at an opportune moment in public.

Case #6

Obi, a middle-aged man, did not get along very well with Oke. In fact they were in covert conflict and regarded each other as enemies, though most people didn't know. Obit sought an opportune moment for revenge and it came one day during a public meeting where many men in the community were discussing community issues in an open forum. Oke stood up and made a sort of ridiculous suggestion to the group. Obi took advantage of the situation to insult Oke in public. He stood up and began his own speech which immediately followed Oke's suggestion by saying: "Nwatà kwùe okwù, à màrà kà ahụ ya ra." (L.T. When a child speaks his maturity is portrayed). He was virtually telling the group that Oke had made a stupid suggestion. This demeaned Oke in public and he sought further opportunities to revenge Obi in return.

An interesting facet of conflict development in Igbo society is a cyclical process wheregy conflicts go from <u>covert</u>--where they are limited primarily to the parties involved or very close kin members/friends only--to <u>overt</u>--where they are openly expressed in full public view. If the latter occurs, then steps are instantly put into motion to reduce or resolve the conflict. Figure 3 illustrates the cyclical nature of covert-overt conflict and vice-versa.

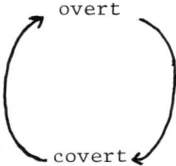

Fig. 3. Conflict cycle

It is clear that the entire process can become quite complicated. An overt conflict can become covert at any time a satisfactory settlement is not reached by both disputants. On the other hand, covert conflicts often reach a point where they explode into overt conflicts, especially through an exchange of words or *iliā olilia*, a verbal duel, which is a highly public affair and draws an audience instantly from the surrounding community because of its loudness and the use of offensive terms. The audience is a key element in this communicative strategy for it serves to increase the quality of performance. An exchange of words consists of a battle between adversaries to defeat the other through ridiculing or shaming the opposing adversary in public. This may be achieved by <u>what</u> is said as well as <u>how</u> it is said. To insult or ridicule is one degree of skill but to do it in quotes or proverbs is an ultimate level, hard to counter and almost always successful. The following account illustrates just how an adversary might effectively humiliate his opponent in public with a proverb during *iliā olilia*.

Case #7

Two young boys, Onyegbuna and Chika, were enemies. One day they began to quarrel. Prior to the quarrel, Chika had taken his school examination and the results were published in the local newspapers. His name did not appear in the newspapers which meant he had failed the exam. During the quarrel that day Onyegbuna remembered this and used this information to insult Chika before the others who were witnessing the quarrel when he told Chika: "Agadi nwanyì dàa n'àlà àgboro àbụ̀ạ, à gụ̀a ihe dì n'àbo yā ōnụ̄." (L.T. If an old woman falls down twice, the things in her basket are counted (by those around her). That is, everyone was looking forward to what he would do the next time he took the exam; and if he failed again everyone would surely laugh at him. This comment made Chika emotionally upset because Onyegbuna had reminded him in public of what the general public already knew. Chika was so overcome by anger that he couldn't respond with any appropriate counter-statement or insult to Onyegbuna so he started to fight him physically, but this only made him appear less intelligent before the others and brought more shame on him.

Because of the inflammatory nature of *iliā olilia* and the focus of Igbo society on the ideal of "stopping things before they get out of hand," other members of the society are expected to intervene to stop the quarrel. They can do this physically by force if necessary, or more commonly verbally by advising or begging one or both parties to discontinue. At this point, a third party becomes advisor in the heat of the verbal duel. Such an adviser might try to convince his friend or relative that the other person may eventually harm him by using a quote: "Ogbū̄ agwọ nà-àchọ ndù̀, agwọ ọ nà-ègbu nà-àchọkwa ǹkè ya." (L.T. A person trying to kill a snake should remember that the snake also wants to live). This is a way of diverting the attention of one adversary to realize that when he tries to harm someone, he should remember that the opponent will in turn try to hurt him.

Iliā olilia often leads to one of the parties trying to intimidate the other which usually consists of promises of future revenge or challenges to a physical fight then and there. Both are strategies to scare off the adversary and thus gain a victory in the exchange of words, since weakness or cowardice can be considered shameful in Igbo society.

Case #8

Two different groups of people were enemies. One day, the group with more people began to threaten the group with less people. The smaller group defended itself from the threats of the larger group by responding: "Òchìcha biagōdū̄ nà pūkū otù nwà òkụkò gà-àtụtụrụchā ha." (L.T. Even if cockroaches come in thousands, one chicken can destroy them all). That is, even if the larger group attacked them, they (smaller group) would defeat them.

However, if the adversary does not back down, a physical fight can ensue as a result of the verbal challenge or other insults. This is fairly rare in the society because of the detrimental consequences that follow for both parties involved, but it is a possibility. If the police are called in, criminal charges are likely and the possibility of a Magistrate's Court case becomes dangerously real.

INTERACTIONAL ROLES AND COMMUNICATIVE STRATEGIES

From the above discussion it is obvious that the participants and their patterns of behavior at each stage in the development of the conflict are characteristically different. The interactional roles of the participants are a key notion to understand exactly which communicative strategies are most successful in managing conflicts and why.[25] In a similar study, Arewa and Dundes (1964: 79) suggest in their pioneering article on the ethnographic study of proverbs that the identity of the participants (speaker, addressee, audience) in the interactional settings in which a proverb is used is the key to explaining the use of proverbs as opposed to ordinary speech as well as the appropriateness of specific proverbs in these settings. In our study, the identity of the participants in the interaction (i.e., interactional roles), which can be defined for each stage of the conflict, is the key to understanding the use of quoting behavior.

Advisor-advisee Roles

Advisor-advisee roles are usually enacted by those who have a close interpersonal relationship based on friendship (if between non-kin members) or kindship. Friends and kin members are obligated to help each other advance as well as warn one another of danger. Giving advice--especially when the advice is not solicited by the advisee--is one example of this obligation. As one Igbo speaker commented: "You instruct somebody on how they should act; you warn somebody of the consequences of their action: look forward and look back and try to know what you are doing." In terms of conflict then, the goal of the advisor is to prevent or reduce conflict development by addressing a comment or criticism to the advisee on his present or future behavior. Since the message amounts to a criticism of the advisee's character and/or behavior, it has the potential of disrupting the close relationship which exists between the two. A skillful advisor can avoid such a disruption by using a proverb which effectively depersonalizes the message and consequently he can avoid implicating himself or the advisee in a personal way. In addition, the proverb by its nature is more powerful and consequently more persuasive. As one Igbo person noted:

> The proverb drives home the advice. It is more persuasive than direct words. If the advisor tells me literally, his advice is not carrying the serious effect the proverb wil carry. It's just very casual and light advice.

In other words, one's own words are not as powerful as a quote and therefore the user is not as successful in achieving his interactional goal.

One illustration of the advisor-advisee role will serve to exemplify quoting of proverbs.

Case #9

> Two men, Okeke and Eze were good friends. Okeke was a trader who sold television sets and other things. Eze wanted to buy

a television set, so he told Okeke that he was interested in
buying a television set. Okeke showed him one television set
but when Eze tested it something did not function well and he
began to suspect that the television might not be in good
condition. Eze told Okeke: "Please, Okeke, you know Ọ̀kụkọ̀
ùkwụ̀ jìrì ànāghī ère ya nà dìàlà." That is, if this television
set is not in good order you had better tell me, since friends
don't cheat friends.

As this illustration indicates, the advisor seemed to have some
indication that the advisee might be doing or about to do something
against the prescriptive mores of the society which could land the
advisee into conflict with himself or another: selling bad merchandise to a friend. To convey these suspicions in an open and
direct manner not only would implicate the advisor but would possibly
have shamed or embarrassed the advisee into a response of anger at
such a suggestion--whether it were true or not. The proverb quoted
in Case #9 presents a potentially insulting message in a non-insulting way. Since the message is depersonalized by the proverb, neither
the speaker nor the addressee is held personally accountable for its
contents and a disruption of interpersonal communication is avoided.
The prestige and power of the quote is a useful verbal strategy to
achieve the goal of altering the advisee's actions. The proverb
more easily persuades the addressee who feels somewhat complimented
that the speaker used a form of speech which only the "intelligent"
and those skilled in the ways of culture could understand. This
along with the chance to save himself gracefully without too much
shame put the advisee in the mood to alter his behavior, and the
conflict is reduced. In short a very personal and sensitive message
and intercommunicative situation has been successfully handled with
the help of a depersonalized communicative strategy--a quote.

Case #10

Two young males, Obi and Okereke, were friends. Obi had a
disagreement with another peer, Nnaka (a male). They became
enemies. One day they were about to fight each other. Since
Nnaka was bigger and could probably have a much better chance
in defeating Obi, Okereke told Obi: "Òke gbabà n'ìgbùdà aka
akpara ya." (L.T. Rats which try to pass through clay traps
usually get caught). That is, Obi shouldn't try to defy a
stronger force because he didn't have the strength to defend
himself against the repercussions that might arise. Remembering that Okereke was his friend who wanted to help him and convinced of the truth of Okereke's depersonalized statement, Obi
withdrew from the fight.

Case #10 occurs at a more excitable stage of conflict development
in which the advisee needs to consider the consequences of his
actions. A skillful advisor uses a proverb in a tense situation
to reduce rather than increase the conflict and thus he avoids
being the brunt of such a hot-tempered situation. The proverb--
because of its prestige value in the culture--has the power to catch
the advisee's attention enough to cool him down and make him aware

of the consequences of engaging in a useless battle. At the same
time the advisor is protected from the implication of an insulting
message because of the depersonalized nature of the message which
holds no one personally accountable, at least not in a personal way.

Offended-Accused Roles

Once one party feels his rights and/or benefits prescribed by the
society have been violated, he begins to enact the interactional
role of an "offended" party. Offenses characteristically consist
of one party's failure to fulfill culturally specified obligations,
such as showing appreciation for a favor or gift, treating certain
members of a group unequally or unfairly, or one party's taking
advantage of another, such as being greedy, trying to implicate
another, soiling another's name. In either case, offended-accused
roles mark a deterioration in interpersonal relationships. Depending upon the degree of this deterioration, the proverb can be used
by the offended (1) to point out the offense to the accused in hopes
of changing his behavior so that the relationship might be restored
or (2) to defend his own integrity, intelligence, and strength as
one who refuses to allow others to take advantage of him. In the
second instance the interpersonal relationship is seriously deteriorated and the proverb is then a means of insulting or intimidating
the accused.

Pointing out the offense serves to change the behavior of the
accused without alienating him; consequently, interpersonal relationships can be restored rather than worsened, since the depersonalized nature of the proverb allows the offended to criticize the
behavior of the accused without specifyin deliberateness. Thus the
conflict can be reduced. Two illustrations of such usage include
Cases #11 and 12.

Case #11

> Chima did a favor for Mmaduka. However, mmaduka did not show
> appreciation for the favor. Later Chima, who felt offended by
> Mmaduka's ingratitude, told Mmaduka, "A dàa elū. à hụ àlà
> mmụo." (L.T. You learn a lesson from a bad experience). That
> is, he had learned a lesson from this and the next time he
> would not offer to help Mmaduka again. Realizing that Chima
> was angry, Mmaduka said nothing at the time but later he re-
> turned to apologize to Chima.

Case #12

> A group of men were having a meeting. Those in charge of the
> meeting were encouraging others there to feel free to speak
> out and to give their own opinions on the matter at hand. But
> when some junior members began freely speaking out, the senior
> man who had encouraged open and free speech began to rebuke
> those junior men who spoke out. Ill-feeling began to arise
> between those being rebuked and those who had encouraged open
> and free speech. A member of the junior group then stood up
> and said: "Onye nà-àkpo nkịta òkù jìri apịpia n'àkà, ọ sị̀ ya

> bìa k'ò sì ya abiàlà." (L.T. One who is calling a dog and
> has a stick in his hand, does he really want the dog to come?).
> He was reminding the senior men of what they had previously
> said, "feel free, feel free to talk" but when they actually
> starting speaking their minds, they were silenced. After that,
> the junior men just sat down and kept quiet even though the
> senior men again tried to urge them to speak out. The junior
> men said nothing since their first attempts to freely speak
> out were not received well.

In both Cases #11 and #12 proverbs convey the reaction of offended parties to an offense in a manner that allows the accused to realize their mistake and change their behavior without in turn feeling insulted or alienated. In addition, the power of the quote serves to make the accused fully aware that the offended party takes the matter seriously.

Cases #11 and #12 also mark what might be called "positive" uses of the proverb in that they seek to save the interpersonal relationship from further deterioration. Proverbs are also used, however, in "negative" ways as retaliation when the offended feels his integrity and intelligence have been challenged by the accused through an act of aggression or that he is being taken advantage of. The latter is a very sensitive issue in Igbo society. Retaliation, then, often takes the form of an insult or intimidation with the use of a proverb, if the speaker is most skillful.

Case #13

> Three male peers, Okonkwo, Uba, and Nwankwo, spent a lot of
> time with each other. Okonkwo and Uba considered each other
> to be close friends, while they considered themselves to be
> only casual friends with Nwankwo. One day while they were
> all three together Nwankwo insulted Okonkwo. Okonkwo then
> turned to his close friend, Uba, while both were in the presence of Nwankwo and said: "Mpàkò nri bùtèrè, ònye sìrì nke
> a?" (L.T. Sharing food brings up the question: Who cooked
> this or that?). That is, he had given Nwankwo the opportunity
> to insult him because he allowed him to keep company with them.
> Nwankwo felt humiliated because he then realized that he had
> never been wholly accepted into the group. (It is not known
> whether the conflict was resolved at that time or continued
> later).

Case #14

> Two female students in a teacher training college, Nneka and
> Ijeoma, were friends. Nneka borrowed a ballpoint pen from
> Ijeoma. Later Ijeoma lost it but did not inform Nneka that
> she had lost it. Nneka came to Ijeoma one day and said she
> needed her pen and would like it back. Ijeoma explained
> lightly that she had lost it and had forgotten to inform
> Nneka. Nneka inquired as to how long ago Ijeoma had lost the
> pen and Ijeoma explained perhaps two or three weeks ago.

Angered that Ijeoma had taken something entrusted to her so lightly and had not even had the courtesy to inform the person who lent it to her that she had lost it, Nneka expressed her disappointment and anger to Ijeoma. Ijeoma did not respond apologetically or by begging for forgiveness but rather treated the whole matter lightly by replying "Isn't it only 10 pennies worth?". Nneka was even more angered by this response and Ijeoma's refusal to apologize for losing the pen. Nneka responded: *"Mbẽ sị nà ozu ọzọ gà-ànwụ."* (L.T. Tortoise said another death would occur). That is, she was writing for the next time when Ijeoma would need something more valuable than a pen and Nneka would refuse to give it to her. As a result of Ijeoma's refusal to be apologetic about her mistake, Nneka and Ijeoma's friendship deteriorated.

It is evident that Cases #13 and #14 aim at more than merely pointing out an offense. The proverb is used to express not only the offended's vexation but also to frighten the accused into changing the actions which are considered so offensive.

Case #13 also involves an additional communicative strategy which adds more pain and injury to the insult. The proverb is addressed indirectly to the accused even though it seems to be directly addressed to a friend and supporter of the offended. This technique which consists of "bouncing" a depersonalized message while also making it seem as if the speaker is gossipping about the person present makes the message even more stinging. The offended person is protected from personal involvement while the accused or now the attacked person has little means to respond. "Bouncing" a quote is a communicative strategy which gives the user double power and double protection from implication.

Adversary Roles

Adversary roles appear at a more advanced stage in conflict development when interpersonal relationships have deteriorated to the point of on-going enmity. At this point each party becomes an opponent in a battle for victory. One of the most common ways this victory is achieved is through the destruction or damage to the opposing adversary's character or reputation--either in public or in private domains. Privately this can be achieved through *imẹbị āhā mmadụ̀* (gossiping and soiling the other person's name). Publicly, this can be achieved at public gatherings during speech making or when a quarrel spontaneously erupts in *iliā olilia* (verbal dueling). *Iliā olilia* amounts to a verbal duel played before a spontaneous audience in which the goal is to use one's verbal skill to shame the opposing adversary in public. The adversary who most effectively humiliates the other by bringing out things which are considered very shameful and by doing so in the most skillful manner verbally is the victor. Case #15 is a good example of how victory can be achieved.

Case #15

Two young boys, Onyegbuna and Chika, were enemies. One day

they began to quarrel. Prior to the quarrel, Chika had taken
his school examination and the results were published in the
local newspapers. His name did not appear in the list of
successful candidates in the newspapers. Everyone knew than
he had failed the exam. During the quarrel that day. Onyegbuna
remembered this and used this information to insult Chika before the others who were witnessing the quarrel when he told
Chika, "Agadi nwanyì dàa n'àlà ùgbòrò, àbùa à gùa ihe dì n'àbọ
yā ōnū." (L.T. If an old woman falls down twice, the things in
her basket are counted by those around her). That is, everyone
was looking forward to what he would do the next time he took
his exam; and if he failed again everyone would surely laugh
at him. This comment made Chika emotionally upset because
Onyegbuna had reminded him in public of what the general public
already knew. Chika was so overcome by anger that he could not
respond with any appropriate counter-statement or insult to
Onyegbuna so he started to fight him physically, but this only
made him appear less intelligent before the others and brought
more shame on him.

Case #15 utilizes a proverb to win a verbal duel and it effectively
does so when the opponent (Chika) cannot retort with an equally or
more insulting proverb or even an ordinary statement. The result
is that Chika is double shamed by the proverb here not only because
the message disgraces him but even more so because Onyegbuna de-
livered it with verbal skill which Chika could not skillfully counter. Thus Chika's inability to counter the proverb portrayed him
as less intelligent adding more insult to the injury incurred by
the message. In short, the proverb here is a clever verbal tool
which allows an adversary to defeat his opponent in public through
abuse while seeming quite innocent of the abuse waged. The defeated
adversary is left to fight a powerful yet invisible weapon while
the victor has achieved what sociologists often refer to an "one
up-manship."

Mediator-disputant Roles

The goal of the mediator is to resolve the conflict between two
disputants through reconciliation during a very common speech
event, idozī okwu or mediation. Mediators are obligated to see
that peaceful co-existence is maintained. They are supposed to be
honest, fair, and impartial in dealing with disputants; hence,
their role is a precarious one, for in order to succeed in making
peace they must convince both disputants to accept their decision.
Since the mediator must often blame one or both disputants and/or
give a judgment, the proverb is a necessary verbal took which can
permit them to hold one or both disputants responsible yet appear
unbiased and neutral in their decision. The authority which the
proverb can add to the mediator's statement as well as its per-
suasiveness in getting disputants to accept this judgment explain
why skillful mediators draw upon proverbs frequently. Case #16
below is one illustration.

Case #16

Two men, Dike and Oko, were friends. They got into a quarrel. Hearing the quarrel, an older male, Imo, rushed in to break up the quarrel and then tried to settle the matter. Imo heard the complaints from Dike and Oko separately. Then, he decided that Dike had caused the quarrel; he advised Dike that what he was doing was wrong: "Mmadù àdighì àma m̀gbè ọ gàfèrè n'ama ibe ọgò ya." (L.T. You never know when you cross into your in-law's compound). That is, one never knows whether the person he is mistreating may some day be closely related to him or even be supervising him at a job, etc.

Case #16 illustrates how the proverb is often used by a mediator to persuade a disputant of the justness of his decision. First, the message of the proverb serves to remind the disputant that his actions do not fall in line with the prescriptive rules of the society. Secondly, by using a quote, such as a proverb, the mediator is able to criticize the behavior of one disputant without alienating him or implicating himself as being biased in his decision. The depersonalization of the proverb at the same time protects the peacemaker from being held personally accountable for a potentially insulting message and it also protects the disputant from being openly shamed to the point that he will not accept the decision. Thirdly, using a prestigious and valued form of speech, the mediator not only affirms his intelligence and prestige to which disputants often owe allegiance but he also indirectly praises the disputants involved by using a proverb. These two qualities put more pressure on disputants to accept the judgment rendered. The disputants are more convincingly persuaded to accept the judgment rendered because the mediator has proven himself authoritative, yet just. They feel complimented and proud that he chose such a prestigious and unshameful way of approaching them. Thus, they are in an optimal mood to accept the decision and abide by it.

As the various cases above illustrate, two immediate or obvious functions are being served by the communicative strategy of using quotes: power and protection. The properties which are typical only of quotes and not of a person's own words combine to produce a more powerful message than ordinary language might convey, yet they also serve to protect the personal integrity of the addressee, in most cases. At the same time, the speaker is obviously protected from implications which he might suffer as a result of the message he conveys. All of this is realized primarily because a quote is a depersonalized statement in a very personal and sensitive interaction. As such, quotes are unique and well-suited communicative strategies to manage conflict at each stage in its development.

SKILL IN COMMUNICATING

Performance ability or skill is another interpretive factor to explain the use of proverbs and their effect in conflict situations. The skill factor is part of role relationships but deserves to be analytically separated for this study because of the central importance of this concept in Igbo society. As evident from the discussion of role relationships, proverbs are a prestigious form of speech which can optionally be used to realize skillful role enactment in conflict situations. That is, skillful role enactment is defined by performance of certain prescribed patterns of behavior and the proverb is one verbal tool which can be utilized to achieve these prescribed patterns of behavior. In addition, the use of proverbs is a skill in its own right in addition to the general interactional skill. The prescribed patterns for the interactional role do not have to be the same as those for the use of proverbs. The skill is the extent to which one knows these patterns and can enact the roles. Therefore, the skill factor will be discussed in terms of: (1) the use of proverbs; and (2) role enactment, in order to offer generalizations on how the two inter-relate as reflected in recalled instances of interaction collected from members of Igbo culture.

The ability to use proverbs appropriately is a mark of "intelligence" and therefore is prestigious in Igbo society. As one bilingual member phrased it: "The common language, any fool can go about it, but the use of proverbs displays your intelligence and maturity in language and experience." It is clear from this comment that this form of speech is highly prestigious and that its use can thus earn the user prestige. However, not everyone in the society is equally skilled in the use of proverbs. Skill ranged from a passive knowledge which includes only being able to understand the interactional meanings and implications of proverbs, to various degrees of active knowledge, which means ability to use proverbs appropriately. The latter minimally includes the following: (1) recall of the exact wording and pronunciation of the proverb; (2) knowledge of the kinds of situations to which the use of this specific proverb applies; and (3) knowledge of the conditions of etiquette under which the use of this form of speech applies in terms of the speaker and addressee(s). Those members of the society who possess the largest inventory of proverbs and the ability to conform to all three of the above types of conditions correctly are noted as having the highest degree of verbal skill in the use of proverbs. An Igbo speaker's comment illustrates this:

> There are a variety of different proverbs appropriate for the same situation. There are people who are vast in that and can select a variety of alternative proverbs for the same occasion. Others know only one. The first is more skillful than the second.

There is a high cultural awareness in Igbo society of the skillful use of proverbs, to the extent that speakers try to use proverbs only when they are certain they have conformed to the three conditions mentioned above and consequently have met the criterion of skill. There are strong informal sanctions in Igbo society against the inappropriate use of proverbs. The inappropriate use of proverbs carries the notion that "when anybody uses any of these proverbs wrongly, he has made stupid of himself," according to one respondent. Therefore, it is fairly rare to find inappropriate or unskillful use of proverbs. As one Igbo respondent put it: "If a person is uncertain, it is better for him not to use the proverb but to say it literally, in plain simple language." This is especially true for members of the society in certain ascribed status positions, such as those defined by sex and age. Skill in the use of proverbs is socially prescribed for certain status positions. Male elders are expected to be more intelligent and mature by virtue of their age which brings them higher status in traditional Igbo society.[26] They are conceived as the link to the ancestors who command the highest respect. The elders are the ancestors of the future. They embody the ancestors in the present through role enactment.

The choice of proverbs as opposed to ordinary or direct language, as well as the ability to use proverbs appropriately and possibly in abundance, are all reflections of the level of intelligence and maturity prescribed for certain ascribed status positions. Thus, an intelligent person is one who is skillful in role enactment and uses verbal skill to realize his goals. In regard to skillful role enactment, one Igbo speaker noted:

> If something were to cause trouble, an intelligent person would use some words to bring calm. That's why intelligent people in the community are often mediators [peacemakers]. They have the ability to cope with people very well, to settle matters, and to speak in a sensible way.

Another comment reflects the interrelationship between intelligence and verbal skill: "Knowing proverbs and using them appropriately means that you are intelligent because it's just like being able to find out something in a textbook or dictionary."

All of these comments suggest why those in higher status positions are penalized more severely than those in lower status positions for unskillful role enactment and unskillful use of proverbs. For example, if a young male uses a proverb unskillfully, i.e., inappropriately, in the presence of elder males, he may simply be corrected; whereas, if an elder male uses a proverb unskillfully or inappropriately in the presence of other elder males, he can be laughed at possibly to the point of scorn. On the other hand, males who do not qualify for high status positions by ascription can qualify by achievement, that is, if they can use proverbs with the degree of skill expected of elders in such a position.

Leadership must always be earned through skillful role enactment, no matter what achieved or ascribed characteristics one might possess. Leadership and consequently authority and prestige can be obtained by using language to maneuver others. Since "influential elders are verbally aggressive, enjoy public speaking, and are good at manipulating others . . . (Ottenberg, 1971: 160), it follows that skilled use of a highly prestigious form of speech, e.g., proverbs, can facilitate skillful enactment of roles to earn one prestige and leadership (see Figure 4).

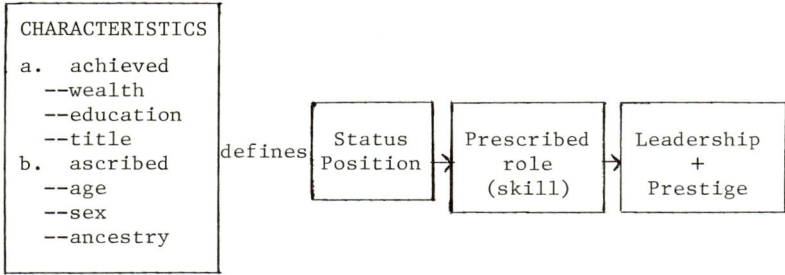

Fig. 4. Relationship between skill, status position, and role

Although leadership in the lineage is ascribed to adult males who attain the proper age, outstanding leaders informally emerge who have at least three personal attributes--all of which reflect skillful performance according to the cultural model: (1) "speaking ability"; (2) knowledge of historical and recent events in the compound or village as well as tradition; and (3) interest in the affairs of the group. As Ottenberg (1971: 303) notes:

> Leadership is a question of the ability of a skillful person to manipulate individuals and groups for his own ends. There is a strong sense of group identity . . . and a successful leader is able to make this work for him.

Thus, in Igbo society leadership positions cannot be obtained without skill in using language and hence the use of proverbs is essential to achieving leadership positions.

NOTES

1. Ethnographic surveys generalizing the entire Igbo society include: Basden, 1921; Meek, 1937; Forde and Jones, 1962; and Uchendu, 1965. For an ethnographic study of one village community in Owerri Province (Umueke in Agbaja village-group) see Green, 1947. For a detailed ethnographic study of the Afikpo community of Igbo society, see Ottenberg, 1968 and 1971.

2. The Owerri Igbo refer to this community as "town," but since the community is rural as opposed to urban, the term village-group as originally adopted by Green and Ottenberg will be utilized in this study.

3. A patrilineage is here defined as a unilineal descent group whose members reckon descent through males to a single male ancestor. There may be wider groups than the patrilineage among the Owerri Ibgo, but insufficient data does not permit this generalization in this study. The Igbo term *ụmụ nnà* in its most general sense refers to the patrilineage kinship group. In its narrowest sense, the same term refers to the children of the same father.

4. *Ọfọ* is a sacred staff made of several pieces of an *òfo* tree wrapped with a wire or string and often covered with the feathers and blood of a chicken which may have been sacrificed over it. *Ọfọ* is the highest symbol of authority among the Owerri Igbo and oaths are sworn on it much as the same as they are on the Bible in Western society. The holder of *òfo* is responsible for ensuring that the customs or *omenàlà* are followed within the lineage group.

5. Compounds are often changing units. Nowadays they may consist of fewer members because of the high degree of friction possible among compound members or perhaps the high density of population among the Owerri Igbo.

6. This is probably due to the influence of Christianity which does not permit its male members to have more than one wife and also to the influence of a money-based economy and consequently other means by which wealth can be acquired and displayed.

7. "Social sentiments" is a term coined by Needham (1962) to refer to the duties and obligations obtaining between different members of a society.

8. <u>Social roles</u> refer to the prescribed patterns of behavior specified by the social structure for certain individuals toward other individuals.

9. Abomination (arṳ) refers to unnatural and abnormal actions which usually are punished by death or abandonment and regarded with disdain; for example, in olden times, the birth of twins, breech birth, or marriage to an òsu by a dìàlà.

10. There is a strong belief among Owerri Igbo that those women who are honest and fair peacemakers and who treat children nicely will be allowed to bear children and vice-versa. Therefore, women try to show their love to all children so that they will in turn bear many children of their own.

11. Exogamy refers to the requirement for marriage outside a defined social category or group.

12. Age sets perform public duties, e.g., clearing paths, cutting forests, and acting as market police. They also provide mutual help to one another and exercise discipline over their own members in cases of misbehavior (Forde and Jones, 1962; 19).

13. The work group is an organization consisting of several males who either hire themselves out to do work for others or work for each other as a group. They have an elected leader and often a secretary and treasurer who keep records. The leader helps to settle conflicts that arise between members. Those for whom the work group works are obligated to provide the group with lunch and refreshments.

14. <u>Progress</u> refers to status advancement through achieved means which may include taking of titles, acquisition of wealth, leadership, formal education, or divination.

15. In "A Comparative Theory of Dispute Institutions in Society," Abel (1975: 220-330) suggests theoretical distinctions which readily fit the folk conception of members of Igbo society. Abel defines "conflict" as "a common developmental stage in any relationship" in which parties develop "inconsistent claims to a resource," whether the resource be tangible, e.g., property rights or intangibles, e.g., one's reputation. "Conflict" is viewed by Abel as a chronological antecedent to "dispute"--another form of social relationship in which inconsistent "claims" are communicated to someone, either the opposing party or a third party. Abel terms "claims"

communicated to the opposing party as "quarrel" or "argument" and "claims" voiced are usually justified in terms of a "norm."

In this essay, conflict encompasses a series of developmental stages which include not only what Abel (1973: 227) refers to as "conflict" but also "dispute." Therefore, here, conflict includes actions which are conceived by members of the culture as leading to any of the stages in the conflict sequence.

16. *Esèmokwu* refers to verbal or physical expression of disagreement or, as Abel (1973) termed it, 'inconsistent claims to a resource being voiced and justified in terms of a norm.' The term *èsèmokwu* literally refers to "stretching or dragging on of speech." This is an accurate description of what *èsèmokwu* involves, for once disagreement is in the process, speech making and verbal aggression continue between the two parties involved as well as between the many supporters of each party. This can go on for long periods of time.

17. Uchendu (1965: 14) notes that to the Igbo 'social justice' is more than law. He is referring to the notion that resolution does not include victory for one of the parties and a loss for the other, but rather a compromise that allows peaceful adjustment of social relations to be the outcome.

18. The highest class of offenses are violations of taboos. These offenses, which include only incest and homicide, are considered abominations not only against another human being but also against supernatural powers and against the earth (*ala*). (Uchendu, 1965: 44). *Nso* require ritual purification because of their supernatural violations.

Unless specified otherwise, "offense" as used in this research refers primarily to offenses which are not *nso* since most of the data centered on non-supernatural offenses.

19. Theft is very much detested in Igbo society. It is dealt with seriously. Usually the thief is exhibited before the community and members of the community pass by cursing, ridiculing and spitting on him.

False accusation is a very serious offense for which one can be tried and penalized. In fact, even a hinted slight on a person's reputation may be penalized (Green, 1947: 93).

20. The folk definition for *iliā olilia* reflects the type of interchange which occurs:

> It's saying things you are not supposed to say to another, because you are angry; you say many things to make the other person feel low and disgraced and make him feel you are nice and good and better than him in every aspect . . . it's mainly done in public or it may begin in private but then the public comes in . . . it's emotionally caused; people may not be conscious of what they are doing.

22. I owe the suggestion for the flow chart using a decision-making model to Paul Garvin. For further information regarding the use of decision-making models to illustrate ethnographic information, see Gladwin, C. (1976) and Garvin (1965).

To simplify matters, the flow chart illustrates only those conflicts which are beginning afresh as opposed to renewed conflicts.

23. With the exception of the use of proper names in place of pronouns and the alteration of the English to a more standard form, all of the illustrations provided are as given by male and female Igbo respondents.

24. One-party mediation consists of the peacemaker approaching one party at a time to try to settle the matter by persuading each party to take a certain step which could eventually result in a compromise. It is often a common approach when the two parties refuse to be brought together because of anger or strong ill-feelings because he does not feel the other party has any claim to make.

25. Role is defined as 'prescribed patterns of behavior' for participants in an interaction or in the society (interpersonal or societal roles). For this study, interactional role is conceived as having a specific function in the conflict sequence.

26. Elders represent the highest living traditional authority (Ottenberg, 1971: 275). Their role centers primarily around settling disputes between villages and within villages, as well as maintaining a sense of unity against the encroachment of external political forces (Ottenberg, 1971: 303-304).

CHAPTER 4
IGBO THEMES

DEFINITION OF "THEME"

The investigation of quoting behavior in Igbo society described in this book reveals certain fundamental aspects about Igbo culture as a whole which extend beyond language usage. These core cultural aspects or "themes" can provide insight into the world view of Igbo society

The theoretical concept of "theme " can be utilized in this study to move from the description to the interpretation of cultural patterns. Conversely, one can then assume that the use of proverbs as here described and analyzed are empirical manifestations or expressions of one or more "themes" of Igbo culture. For this study, "theme" has been conceived as a generalization about a culture expressed by regularities in many aspects of the culture.[1] The concept of "theme" was originated by Opler (1945: 198) who defined it as: ". . . a postulate or position, declared or implied, and usually controlling behavior or stimulating activity, which is tacitly approved or openly promoted in a society." Thus, themal analyses seek the underlying principles on which members of a society operate, i.e., the criteria internal to the culture in question.[2] Opler's concept is particularly helpful in interpreting reflections of Igbo culture because "language . . . one of the aspects of culture, is especially well-suited to reveal what is meant by a theme, how themes are related to one another, and how they are related to the particulars of culture" (Zamora, et al., 1971: 221).

There are at least three basic themes in Igbo culture which can be inferred from the use of proverbs in conflict situations.[3] These themes which are intricately interrelated are expressed by other aspects of the culture as well. Often all three underlie the use of proverbs in conflict situations. Of interest to the ethnography of speaking in Igbo society is that many other linguistic resources besides proverbs are utilized to express some of these three basic themes.

Theme #1: Skillfulness in Being Indirect

"Being indirect" most often means depersonalizing a very personal and consequently sensitive communicative situation. As exemplified in the previous discussion of quoting behavior, theme #1 manifests itself in an emphasis on role enactment or the skillful performance in handling others in very sensitive communicative situations as well as in the use of language, specifically proverbs.

As the previous ethnographic discussion suggested, there is a great deal of appreciation in Igbo society for indirectness, whether this is manifested in verbal or non-verbal ways. Deporsonalization is apparently a necessary verbal manifestation of indirectness. Quoting is probably one of the most common verbal means of depersonalization, at least for adult males. There are other means of depersonalization--both verbal and non-verbal, which will be described in more detail later.

It is obvious that a strong emphasis is placed on skillful performance in depersonalization as manifested in quoting behavior since skill implies knowledge of the ideal cultural mores in theory and practice. Behavior which does not conform to the standard, traditional model is usually open to criticism which can be felt by the receiver as embarrassing or insulting to the extent of beginning or renewing conflict. Communicating such a message in a depersonalized way serves then as a means of internal social control by which behavior is sanctioned in a social setting in various ways depending upon the societal roles involved and the tools used to effect this sanction.

Quoting is not the only means of indirectness in Igbo society. There are a variety of other strategies used to communicate indirectly and depersonalize very personal messages. For example, less prestigious means of verbal indirectness, is *ikpē ìkpè*, i.e., "to speak in general statements." The folk term for this act of speech conforms to the restriction against calling a person's name when criticizing or demeaning that person in public. Mentioning a person by name would amount to an accusation and is therefore a very serious matter. *Ipkē ìpkè* refers to general statements which may be metaphorical, idiomatic, or even proverbial. These statements refer indirectly to others who are present.⁴ *Ime akaja* refers to careless or impolite use of language by resorting to similar forms as used in *ikpē ìkpè* but without circumspection; it is therefore often offensive to those referred to who are present.⁵

Another linguistic resource is the folktale or prose narrative which is popular and in abundance in Igbo society. It is commonly used in place of proverbs to convey a similar message or stress a point. In fact, some proverbs stem from folktales and thus represent capsule versions of folktales. For example, *"Mbè sì nà ozu ọ̀zọ ga-ànwụ"*

(Tortoise said another death will occur.). The philosophical
translation might render something like: 'Some day your need will
occur again and I will refuse to help you.' Another example, "Òke
sòrò ngwèrè m̀aa mmiri, mmiri koō ngwèrè, ò gaghī àko òke." (If the
rat follows the lizard into the rain, they both get drenched but
the water dries off the lizard easily while it doesn't dry off the
rat.) The philosophical meaning is: 'People shouldn't follow
those who are in different social positions than themselves or they
may end up in trouble.'

Further research needs to be done on whether the folktale--as some
have suggested (Peters, 1971)--serves as an alternative linguistic
resource to the proverb to convey a similar message when the speakers
are restricted by their societal role from using proverbs.

Creating songs which voice complaints about higher status members
of society, e.g. men, may be Igbo women's use of indirectness. Nwoga
(1971: 34) notes that women's associations commonly use satire[6] in
singing and dancing to express disapproval and secure demands.
He also suggests that satire is an integral part of ritual in Igbo
society in which proverbs and other linguistic forms are used by
women when singing to ridicule other members of the society they
would not normally be allowed to criticize in other social settings.
Thus,

> Satire then is a form of verbal attack directed against indivi-
> duals or groups who have offended either through personal injury
> or through breaking mores of the community, distinguished from
> curse and spell only because these latter call for some super-
> natural powers to inflict harm on the victim while satire works
> directly on the spirit of the victim (Nwoga, 1971: 37).

Satire has also traditionally been utilized by younger men in masked
dances. Ottenberg (1971: 176) notes that in the Igbo community of
Afikpo, young men present skits in which they openly critize and make
fun of their seniors in a way they could never do at public meetings.
In many Igbo communities, the masked dancers create songs which criticize and ridicule the behavior of higher status members which has
not conformed to the ideal cultural mores. The satire they utilize
is particularly effective because the elders or other members of the
society being criticized or ridiculed are not supposed to show hos-
tility in public toward those who criticize them in this ceremonial
manner; rather, they are supposed to laugh at the humor and creativi-
ty of the songs (Ottenberg, 1971: 177).

Whether used by women in women's dance or by younger males in masked
dances or skits, satire may serve both as a verbal criticism of
behavior and as an outlet for tensions in the community by those
whose societal role does not normally permit such stringent social
comments in most social settings.

Another more recently developed communicative means of indirectness
exists among the more Westernized students at the college and university level. They have acquired the habit of making comments about

the social behavior of peers deemed inappropriate. They utilize cartoons to make this comment. "Cartooning" refers to contracting an art student to draw a picture in somewhat exaggerated style to comment on behavior which does not conform to the mores of the university or college community. This cartoon is then placed at a location where the majority of students gather, more probably the bulletin board outside a refectory (dining room). Such cartoons draw crowds of on-lookers who come to laugh and somewhat scorn the action portrayed in the cartoon. For example, although it may be acceptable outside the confines of a college campus for males to urinate along the road or almost anywhere conspicuous, it is not acceptable behavior on the campus grounds. One male medium-aged student had not yet learned this custom and made the mistake of urinating somewhat in the open on the campus grounds. The next day a cartoon was placed on the bulletin board in full view of everyone which depicted a male standing directly in front of the Provost's (President's) office with a greatly enlarged penis and urine spouting out towards the door of the Provost. Such was the social comment conveyed by this cartoon through pictoral rather than verbal means, yet equally effective in being indirect in social comment. Such cartoons are regular occurrences on college and university campuses. We can assume they serve as means of social control in the same way that verbal resources described above serve in village settings.

In summary we are suggesting that a variety of linguistic or non-linguistic forms in Igbo society--including proverbs--serve as agents of social control. The question as to whether similar linguistic resources in other African or even Western societies are utilized to fulfill the same social function needs to be explored.[7] Along with this question, it would be interesting to explore to what extent similar linguistic resources, e.g., satire, proverbs, and folktales, fulfill the social function of social control in other African societies.

Theme #2:   Prevention or Control of Upsetting Forces

This theme is based on a strong belief in Igbo society that upsetting forces can and should be controlled. Since democratic principles are an important basis on which the Igbo social group operates, control is usually conceived to mean "manipulation" as opposed to coercion or force. Thus in this culture prestige and respect is given to those who act as diplomats rather than as warriors or policemen. Uchendu (1965: 13) has referred to Theme #2 as "maintenance of social and cosmological balance" which is constantly being threatened or disturbed by natural and social events.

The theme of controlling upsetting forces includes both preventing and avoiding those things which could bring disruption in the society. Theme #2 was clearly expressed at almost every stage of conflict development. In fact, the goal of most interactional roles was to prevent conflict development or to control upsetting forces of conflicts already in progress through resolution. Skillful role enactment used proverbs as instruments in achieving this goal because proverbs enabled manipulation of others in the most diplomatic way and consequently resulted in a readjustment of social relations.

Although prevention or control of conflicts is a very predominant theme in the culture, it is an ideal which in reality often does not materialize. Conflicts arise easily in reality because of the sensitivity of members of the culture toward how they are treated. It also seems that the manner in which things are done is as important or more so than what is actually done. This is reflected in the use of language where the manner (form of speech) in which things are said is very important and sometimes even takes precedence over what is said; the use of proverbs is a classic illustration of this. One could assume that the theme of conflict control is of crucial importance and predominance because conflicts tend to arise easily and are frequent in Igbo society.

The theme of prevention varies from the Western focus on intention. In Igbo society, "good intention" is recognized but the emphasis is on prevention. It is one's actions which determine his guilt or innocence--not his intentions. To affirm one's innocence, one must convince those settling the dispute that he took all the necessary steps to prevent the serious outcome for which he is being held accountable. For example, those who are responsible for and have authority over others, such as elders or parents, are held accountable for the trouble or problems gotten into by those over whom they have responsibility. If a son or an entire village is taken to court the parents or village elders are immediately approached and questioned by others as to what steps they took to prevent this from happening or what advice they rendered their charges to save them from this dreadful outcome.

Case #10 illustrates a common proverb which is used by a senior to a junior male to remind him of this theme of prevention. The proverb served as advice to Chidozie to change his actions so as to avoid getting involved: "the relative was telling him he was at fault because everytime something happened he was present."

Intelligence is closely connected to the theme of prevention or control of upsetting forces. Intelligence in Igbo society is a matter of prevention, since it takes intelligence to foresee what can lead to trouble and to stop such actions. This is acutely reflected in the following folk comments on intelligence collected from an elder member of Igbo society:

> . . . an intelligent person can prevent something bad from happening . . . in the community, he is often the mediator in cases.

Intelligence in Igbo society is also a matter of controlling upset forces which is only achieved through skillful performance in manipulation of the culture and the language. The following folk comments reflect this:

> If something causes trouble, an intelligent person uses words to bring calm; he is able to cope with people very well to

settle matters, to speak in a way that is sensible . . . to
analyze things, to handle matters on the spur of the moment in
a nice way.

If something bad happens, an intelligent person can suggest
constructive measures to check it.

Intelligence is often dictated by the way you speak and the way
you give speeches.

Uchendu (1965: 13) notes that Theme #2 is also expressed in Igbo
society by the manipulation of deities or spiritual forces to control an upset in natural events, e.g., death, taboo breaches, etc.
The balance of forces is achieved through such rituals as divination, sacrifice, and appeal to the ancestors.

Theme #3: Collective Conscience is Stressed

In Igbo society, identity is achieved through groups, whether this
be the family, the community, village, or an association, such as
an improvement union, *dibia* association, title societies, age-groups,
or women's dance groups. Because meaning in life is based on communal or group-oriented values (Olisa, 1971: 227), members of Igbo
society have a collective rather than individual-oriented conscience.
One's reputation or "character" is heavily guarded and maintained.
This is why accusations and *imebị āhā mmadù* ("ruining people's
names") are very serious in this society, for they can seriously
damage one's identity which rests and is defined by institutionalized
groups. Consequently, shame and ridicule are serious sanctions of
behavior. "There is nothing an Igbo dreads more than ridicule,"
according to one respondent. The fear of it can prevent deviancy
from the cultural model in many instances.

Group identity puts forth heavy pressure on the members of the culture to conform to the ideal cultural mores and penalizes those who
fail to do so. One of the most severe forms of punishment a community can use is ostracism because it deflates an individual's
identity and the basis on which one's very essence is defined.

The theme of group identity was reflected constantly in role enactment and the use of proverbs in conflict situations. For example,
skillful enactors of the adversary role utilized this theme to heap
serious abuses on their adversaries. They strengthened their abuse
by shaming or ridiculing their opposing adversary in "public," i.e.,
before an audience. In Cases #6 and #7 the theme of group identity
was skillfully used by one adversary to sting his opponent. The
fact that a proverb was used to achieve this goal brought even more
success.

An understanding of Theme #3, collective conscience, explains why
various linguistic resources serve as very effective means of social
control in Igbo society. These resources, which are usually enacted
in public settings, exploit the concept of group identity to its
fullest and thus successfully persuade or shame deviants to conform

with the cultural model.

Group solidarity and reciprocity are also expressions of the theme of group identity. Each group member has rights and obligations owed to his fellow group members. The more money one has, the more one owes to his fellow members; the higher one's status position in the society, the more one is obligated to group members. Prestige comes only through fulfillment of these obligations. Those who dodge fulfilling these obligations are scorned since wealth is a respected and a desired status symbol, but it does not bring the owner prestige unless he shares it with his group members. The good fortune of a group member is delighted in by the other group members because they consider it their own. The sharing of wealth is clearly illustrated in family groupings by the "training of one's brothers and sisters." i.e., seeing that they get established in life by paying school fees or other expenses. It is also illustrated by donating generously to community groups at ceremonial occasions. It is by virtue of the <u>group</u> that Igbos advance their status and they are expected to utilize this and any other good fortune to in turn advance the group.

NOTES

1. This is similar to Benedict's notion of culture: "A culture, like an individual, is a more or less consistent pattern of thought and action" (Benedict, 1934: 46).

2. Opler (1945: 198) viewed his concept of "theme" as similar to the "value attitude" of Talcott Parsons as illustrated in <u>The Structure of Social Action</u> and also Kluckhohn's (1952) "cultural configuration."

3. The three themes suggested here are not intended to be an exhaustive list of all possible themes in Igbo culture, but rather only those which can be inferred from the data collected for this research.

4. The following are some of the folk definitions for *ikpē ìkpè*:

> Using words that refer to certain people without mentioning their names . . . making references but not calling the person's name when you address it to people.

> You don't say it directly to them . . . you just make general statements.

5. The following are some of the folk definitions for *ime akàjà*:

> Using words carelessly or freely, sometimes without very serious inference to sort of abuse another . . . not using the appropriate or polite words.

6. Women are less formally organized than men. Age sets often form associations in which the main activity is singing and dancing as a group for different festive occasions. They try to keep peace among

themselves, and in some cases they also set up loan associations. Other than through the family grouping, this is the primary way that women collectively participate in the village group.

7. Bascom's (1965) suggestion that verbal art is vital to the maintenance of stability and continuity of culture because it enforces "conformity to the accepted cultural norms through the expression of social approval and disapproval of individual behavior" may hold the key to understanding social control in those societies which rely primarily on interaction patterns rather than explicit judicial institutions to achieve social control. It is possible that quoting behavior and other types of verbal art serve a crucial function of social control in such societies.

CHAPTER 5
COMMUNICATING IN QUOTES AROUND THE WORLD

QUOTING BEHAVIOR AMONG BILINGUALS

Although this book has focused primarily on Igbo proverbs, we must recognize that in the Igbo social context where quoting behavior has such a deep social significance, there are many other types of quotes used. Educated members of the Igbo ethnic group are bilingual (Igbo/English) to some degree or even multilingual. Even uneducated members of the Igbo ethnic group have some acquaintance with Pidgin English and in this sense are to some degree bilingual or even multilingual as well. Thus, quoting behavior is no doubt expressed in a variety of different languages depending upon the appropriate social context. Literary, proverbial, or Biblical quotes are cited in English by those who have studied English. Some of the more frequently heard quotes in English include:

"Uneasy lies the head that wear the crown."

"How heavily has the mighty fallen."

"Don't be deceived by outward appearances."

"Out of the abundance of the heart the mouth speaketh."

A word of caution must be given in regard to the use of the English quotes. Because they are used by bilinguals and because a different ethnic group is involved, we cannot assume that they have the same interpretation in Igbo society as in British or American societies. It is obvious that their rules of use are quite different, primarily because of the factor of bilingualism. In Igbo society English quotes can be used in a primarily English speaking setting or interjected at some point in a primarily Igbo speaking setting. Very fluent bilinguals and skilled speakers try to paraphrase Igbo proverbs with English quotes to add force and power to their message. After all, the use of an English quote adds international prestige by its very nature and thus enhances the rhetorical quality of the user.

Literary quotes are connected with formal education in Igbo society. They are perceived as prestigious markers of a well-learned and highly educated person, in the Western sense. Biblical quotes are associated with the religious institution of Christianity but often serve as substitutes or paraphrases of Igbo proverbs. This researcher once attended a church service which was entirely preached in the Igbo language, since all members present were members of the Igbo ethnic group, except the researcher. In the middle of the sermon, the priest interjected an English quote to make his point by saying: '(As the white people say) "Familiarity breeds contempt."' Even though a large majority of the people present were not balanced bilinguals, they no doubt had heard this commonly-used quote enough to understand it as one unit.

In another case observed, a fluent bilingual wanted to convince his college president to refund all the expenses he had accumulated while on a business trip. The procedure of that educational institution for handling such matters was slightly ambiguous, leaving much of the decision up to the authority in charge. Finally, the authority agreed to pay only for the hotel accommodations. The entire exchange up to this point was conducted in English, since this was a rather formal situation. Once the employee understood that he had got as much as he would get and that pursuing the matter might be useless, he responded bilingually with: *"E kwùzìere ēwū, ya àmụo nnē."* L.T. Speak well of a goat and she will produce females, or as the English people say: "Speak the truth and shame the devil." Thus, the employee used a bilingual quoting response to make his point. This no doubt brings a great deal of prestige since it requires a high degree of skill in two languages, one of which brings a very traditional orientation and one of which is associated with Western and modernization. To paraphrase with an English quote reflects a strong degree of bi-culturality which is very much valued in Igbo society.

Although our research did not specifically examine English quotes used in Igbo society, it would be interesting to research to what extent English quotes serve the same social functions as Igbo quotes among members of the Igbo ethnic group. There is some indication that perhaps both English and Igbo quotes share the same inherent functional properties since they can be viewed as different surface manifestations of the same verbal behavior. Especially important is the fact that quotes certainly serve to protect users from implications that their own words might involve. An example taken from a Nigerian newspaper article can illustrate the importance of this protection.

> There apparently was a disagreement between the Roman Catholic priest and members of his parish in one Igbo village community. This community was in the process of practicing a cult in honor

of the New Yam Festival. This cult was very traditional to
the community, but the priest had placed a ban on it, which
was not uncommon in regard to many cults. The priest declared
that any members of his parish found practicing such cult
would be expelled from the parish. Furthermore, the priest
was putting a great deal of pressure on the Chief of the community to stop the cult. According to the newspaper reporter,
the Chief was not available for comment, but another prominent
member of his household was quoted as saying: "Render unto God
what is God's and unto Caesar what is Caesar's."

The above example is an obvious example of a Biblical quote used to express a potentially implicating message in a non-implicating way. The quoter did not want to be held responsible for the content of the message, yet he wanted to say something of value and importance. The result is the use of a Biblical quote.

Literary quotes are also often used to embellish speeches, for example, to introduce a speech or to make a point in a speech. For example, the investigator observed the father of a bride introduce his speech at his daughter's wedding reception with: "Shakespeare said, 'The greatest day in his life was the day he convinced a girl to marry him.'" He was expressing his joy in the marriage of his daughter while also informing the groom that he should be happy to be marrying his daughter. All of this was achieved through a literary quote.

Observations of bilinguals in Igbo society suggest that literary quotes are most commonly used in speech-making as opposed to conflict.

UNIVERSALITY

Quoting behavior is probably universal since it affords societies the opportunity of saying something which is extremely sensitive and personal in a very depersonalized or indirect manner. However, not all societies value this type of verbal behavior equally and certainly there is wide variety in rules of usage or the ethnography of speaking or of quoting from society to society throughout the world. For some reason it appears that the highly urbanized societies tend to rely less and less on quoting behavior. The United States is a good example. One can find older or more rural American English speakers who actually have used quotes, specifically proverbs, in their daily life. These people are capable of citing the social contexts and actual examples of how to quote. Urban-raised Americans can rarely do this unless they are members of specific ethnic groups where this behavior still continues. Even Mukařovský noticed the trend of a sort of decline in quoting behavior with a rise in urbanization, but he offered no explanation. To what extent urbanization is or is not correlated with quoting behavior throughout the world remains to be investigated. It certainly offers an interesting topic in the area of change in language usage and social change.

Of relevance to most of this book is the observation that interactional settings involving conflict seem to be one of the most common social settings in which quoting behavior is manifested throughout the world. In a vast review of other studies of oral literature in Africa, Finnegan (1970: 398-420) notes that many different African societies use proverbs in disputes or legal proceedings to smooth social friction and help individuals adjust to their social role or social position. She notes some specific ways in which counsellors and judges use proverbs in court, for example. Messenger (1959: 64-73) notes also that among the Anang Ibibio--neighbors to the members of the Igbo ethnic group--proverbs are commonly used in law cases or disputes to influence judges in the decisions reached. Bergsma (1970: 151-163) notes that proverbs are used among the Tiv in conflict situations as a means of social control. For example, he cites cases of disputes where proverbs are used to signal to an opponent as well as the audience that an end is sought to the dispute. The opponent can then agree and seek an end to the dispute or he can continue the dispute and be fought.

To this researcher's knowledge, no ethnographic study has yet been conducted on the use of proverbs or other quotes in judicial proceedings, especially in African societies. This is apparently a rich field which could offer important information for African societies in the process of modernizing their judicial proceedings. There are reports that proverbs are commonly used as precedents when arguing a case much the same way Western lawyers use prior "cases" as precedents (Arewa and Dundes, 1964: 70). The ethnographic details of using quotes as precedents remain to be investigated as well as its importance in African judicial processes. An understanding of this behavior in the courtroom could be very useful in fashioning the court system to adapt to African culture rather than impose Western norms and standards.

It need not be assumed that quoting behavior in conflict situations is particular only to African societies. As mentioned previously, Greenhouse (1977) describes how Biblical quotes are commonly used to avoid court cases in a white community in a suburban town in Georgia, USA. In this American community where open conflict is a sign of character flaw, Biblical quotes and other linguistic resources are used to produce resolutions and obviate open expression of conflict.

Occasionally, one can observe quoting behavior used in the media in Western societies, such as, the United States. Usually, they are used to avoid implication or perhaps just as an exemplification of creative writing. The following usage was observed in a news report over the radio. The researcher has paraphrased the ideas conveyed, but the quote stands in its original form.

> The Cleveland teachers are still on strike because the pay increases they are demanding have not been forthcoming. When asked about such demands, a top administrator, Superintendent Smith, explained that the school system was virtually broke and could in no way take a pay increase for 5,000 teachers.

> His final word was: "We certainly would like to increase their pay but you can't squeeze blood out of a rock."

This administrator made his point with a proverb.

In other rural-oriented culture in the United States one can find other examples of proverb usage in potential conflict situations. The following two examples were offered by educators from East Texas and Arkansas.

> One day a man was teaching a class. Something happened between him and his student. He took the student to the principal and the principal and teacher had a private conference. The teacher wanted the student to receive heavy punishment for his offense, but the principal, who was wiser and older, felt it was excessive punishment for the crime. His way of sort of refusing to carry through with what he felt was unfair punishment was to tell the teacher: "Joe, don't ever hire an elephant to step on a flea." Joe then realized the excess of his request and left.

The above example illustrates many of the functional properties suggested at the beginning of this book in that the school principal affectively conveys a rather personal and sensitive (potentially embarrassing) message in a very depersonalized and indirect way. Thus, the teacher is saved some embarrassment and the principal has achieved his goal: to settle the matter in a way which is just and fair to both parties.

> One day a teacher got upset with his principal. It seems the principal was taking a class at night and needed to collect some data for a research paper in his class. He was too embarrassed to tell his teachers the true reason for requesting them to fill a questionnaire out, so instead he told them this was all part of their job and they were expected to do this. Apparently he was viewed as arrogant and slightly stupid by his teachers. Most of them got upset and some resisted filling out the questionnaire only to get a severe reaction from the principal. After a sort of verbal squabble between one teacher and the principal, this same teacher left the principal's office and angrily walked down the hall. As he was walking he met a fellow teacher who knew about the problem. He said him: "Jack, don't ever compromise with ignorance. It'll whip you every time." That's all he said. He made no other comment. This got some anger off his chest while also conveying his feeling about the principal to a colleague and yet he didn't get himself into trouble.

The above example illustrates again the quote's potential to keep the user out of trouble. The depersonalized quality of the quote is most useful in this respect, it seems.

As the few American English examples cited above illustrate, quoting behavior around the world serves to depersonalize a very personal situation. It is, perhaps, this quality which influences the dynamics of quoting in everyday life and also which is shared more than any other quality worldwide.

Some anthropologists have suggested that proverbs serve to release tensions in an acceptable way and as a result confrontation can be avoided. Evans-Pritchard (1963: 226) notes that the Azande use an oblique and "veiled" form of speech (*Sanza*), which includes the notion of proverb, in a malicious way to sting their opponent while sounding quite innocent of the harm they have done. The harmed opponent is thus less able to make overt trouble since the malicious comment is concealed by this form of speech.

In Maninka society proverbs serve as a verbal strategy which allows the exercise of authority in a way that does not imply criticism or manifestation of power--both of which can apparently lead to direct confrontation in Maninka society according to Bird and Shopen (n.d.: 25). In summary we might say that even when conflict may be overt and institutionalized as in Western-like judicial proceedings which are found in more highly organized African states, they play a part in formalizing and controlling the conflicts involved (Finnegan, 1970: 412).

FUTURE RESEARCH

This book and the research on which it is based raises a series of questions for future research. First, to what extent does this ultimate function of increasing skill role performance also apply to other interactional settings not involving conflict in Igbo society? From unanalyzed data collected, it is our impression that the ultimate function of increasing skillful role performance applies also to other interactional settings including the use of a quote to reinforce message-content. To what extent quotes used to reinforce a message function like quotes used to comment on behavior do, remains to be determined.

To what extent are the functions of quoting behavior inferred from data on Igbo society similar to that of quoting behavior in other African and non-African societies? In other words, could it be possible that quoting behavior by its nature has a set of universal functions which are manifested differently in different societies? It seems logical that each society in which quoting behavior exists attach different values and perhaps roles to this behavior. As long as the values and orientation of societies are different, the role of a particular verbal behavior in the life of the members of that society will reflect this difference.

What about the functional properties of quotes discussed in this paper? Could they possibly be universals? Since the nature of quoting behavior itself is defined by these properties, it is very likely that these may be universals. Discussions with some members of Mexican society regarding quoting behavior in that society reveal some similar properties. However, much more comparative work needs to be done to get an insight into this question. It is possible that these functional properties may serve as a useful theoretical framework for quoting behavior which may apply in varying degrees, to quoting behavior of the society at hand. For example, the prestige property for Mexican proverbs in traditional Mexican society may not be as high as the prestige property for Igbo proverbs in traditional Igbo society.

Since quoting behavior has been defined more or less in terms of function, what is the range of different ways it can be manifested in different societies? How do these different manifestations affect the functioning of the behavior in that society, if at all? These and many other questions are left for future study of quoting behavior in the societies around the world.

APPENDIX A
GLOSSARY OF IGBO TERMS

àlà: the earth deity who is considered to be a prominent spiritual force in controlling morality and is believed to be offended if native law and custom are violated.

àmàmihe: literally the knowledge of something or "intelligence." Knowing and applying the laws of the land and being able to use the appropriate strategies to achieve one's goal.

arụ: abominations. Unnatural and abnormal actions which are usually punished by death or societal abandonment.

dìàlà: free-born. Members of a social group who are not descendants of slaves.

ebe nzūko: the central meeting place of a village-group which serves as a ritual, political, and market center.

èsèmokwu: literally the dragging of words; a disagreement that is going to result in "case making."

ezè: chief; leader of the village (now a recognized leader of his community).

èzi: compound; each patrilineage in the village shares one or more distinct and densely populated living quarters called èzi.

ichō okwu: trying to provoke another by words or actions.

idozī okwu: mediation; seeking to reach a compromise and make two disputants discontinue their dispute and live in peace.

idṵ odṵ: giving advice; helpful instructive suggestions to another on how they should act.

igbā àsìrì: gossiping; discussing somebody in a bad way.

igbā ìzù: conferring to decide which party is wrong.

Ìgbò: (same as *Ibo* in older literature); a cohesive social group in southeastern Nigeria of about 10 million or more.

ikā ụkà: case-making; the process of pursuing a dispute or causing trouble which may finally lead to court.

ikō onù: a more intensive degree of *iliā olilia*; a verbal exchange of insults which extend beyond the topic of dispute.

ikpē ìkpe: court settlement; finding out who is wrong and punishing him.

ikpē ìkpè: making general or indirect statements to refer to certain people without mentioning their names.

ikwū okwu: speaking; expressing your mind verbally.

iliā olilia: an exchange of words in a bitter way in public; a verbal duel of insults usually on the topic of a dispute and always before an audience.

ilu: proverb.

imā òdùma: giving conditions; it's a type of advice you give when you feel somebody is not listening and is going contrary to what you way.

imebī āhā mmadù: malicious gossip; misrepresenting other people's names negatively.

imenye egwù: intimidating or frightening another.

itū ìkpè: gossip in proverbs or general statements.

mbara: a common meeting place of a village.

mkpari: abuse or insult; ridiculing another.

nnànnà: ancestors.

nsọ: taboo or supernatural offense of which the most dreaded include incest, and the stealing of yams, sheep, or kola nuts.

òbi: a small hut located near the entrance of a compound where male family members entertain their guests and where worship and sacrificial rituals take place.

Glossary of Igbo Terms 95

ọ̀fọ: a staff using several short thick twigs from a sacred tree which symbolizes authority of the ancestors and is held by the eldest male member of the kindred. Oaths are sworn on ọ̀fọ much the same as they are on the Bible in Western society.

ogọ̀: in laws; husband and his patrilineage are in-laws to the patrilineage of his wife.

omenàlà: literally means "what happens on the land" and encompasses native law and custom that have been transmitted from generation to generation within Igbo society prescribing the ethics on which societal norms are based. A violation of these customary laws is believed to cause dire consequences of a group-enforced or supernatural nature.

Òṇitshà: both a town and former Province in Igboland. In this book Òṇitshà refers to an historical socio-political stronghold having developed a characteristic type of Igbo language and cultural customs which contrast with Owerri in some ways.

onye isi ezī: head of the compound or family unit.

òsu: members of a class-based social group who are descendants of cult slaves who had been sacrificed to a deity generations ago.

Òwèrrì: both a town and former Province in Igboland. In this book Òwèrrì refers to an historical socio-political stronghold having developed a characteristic type of Igbo language and cultural customs which contrast with Òṇitshà in some ways (now capitol of Imo State of Nigeria, February 13, 1976).

ụmụ̀ di: children of the same father but may be of different mothers.

ụmụ̀ nnà: literally means "children of the father" and is used in referring to members of the same kindred in its broadest sense.

ụmụ̀ nnē: children of the same mother.

APPENDIX B
SELECTED PASSAGES FROM MUKAŘOVSKÝ (1971)

Translated by P. L. Garvin

p. 277

Mention of the semantic consequences implies for the proverb the circumstance that it is not usually perceived as an independent semantic whole but rather as part of a broader context.

p. 285

It has almost completely been neglected that the proverb lives--and particularly under present-day circumstances where it has almost entirely lost its didactic value--a complete life only in context. It is lost in context to such an extent that it is sometimes difficult to differentiate it from the surrounding sentences; this occurs particularly if it is placed amidst sentences that just like the proverb have a generalizing meaning, but are formed ad hoc for the particular occasion. Examples will be given later when the generalizing character of the proverb will be discussed in more detail. Another connection between proverb and context is formed by the circumstance that proverbs are closely related to sayings so that sometimes a minute grammatical change is sufficient in order for a proverb to change into a saying or conversely . . . the close relation between saying and proverb serves to link the proverb to the context because a saying which is only exceptionally an entire sentence and usually just a clause member (such as a predicate) is incomplete without the context. A proverb is sometimes dissolved in a context in such a manner that it is quoted only partially--the unuttered residue is in these cases given either by the general knowledge of the proverb in question or by the sense of the contect. It should be added that the

Selected Passages from Mukařovský (1971)   97

p. 285

very fact of partial quotation may be intentional from the point of view of the overall semantic intent of the context, particularly in a context of 'dialogue.' The portion of the dialogue that has not been cited acquires a character of hidden or secret meaning and this secretion of meaning may for instance have the function of a euphemism (particularly if the entire text would from the standpoint of the overall intent of the context sound too vulgar or insulting to a partner). At other times a partial omission of the wording of a proverb can have the intent to involve the listener (in the dialogue, the partner) a little more closely into that sense which the speaker puts into the context. By assuming that the proverb is known to both parties one can indicate that to that extent both parties are in accord with regard to the matter at hand and it is enough to talk about it in allusions: this brings about the allusion--of course only an allusion--that the sense of the context is the same for both parties that are involved in a given speech event.

The proverb, however, is not linked to the context only as one of its components but tries by various means to develop a context from itself. One of these means is for the proverb to create a context from within its own core of meaning. This is attested by the accounts recorded by folklore collectors showing the creation of a certain proverb--these are usually anecdotal . . .

The most effective connection between a proverb and its context is shown by the effect of the context on the semantic aspect of the proverb. The examination of this effect is the actual purpose and goal of our study. We shall not deal with it at this point in detail; it is enough to say that in spite of its apparent formal and semantic completeness a proverb in and of itself is semantically incomplete, it is

p. 287

semantically incomplete, it is ambiguous and only the incorporation into a context determines its sense [meaning]--this determination by context can sometimes quite substantially change the very semantic basis of the proverb.

The latest research has begun to show that life in our present-day society, including our urban society, is filled with products that are analogous to folk creation in the traditional sense of the term. It was shown that on the one hand the old folkloric creations go on living and pass on into a new environment, albeit with some change of function; on the other hand there also arise new creations which the authentic folklore in the usual conception (thus for instance the collective acceptance, the anonymity that is linked to it, the traditional clichés of form and content, etc.).

98   Appendix B

p. 293

> The features of the proverb are divided into three groups in line with three basic aspects . . . they are: first, features having to do with the relation between the proverb and the subject [speaker], particularly the subject that is the originator of the utterance. Second, features characterizing the internal, semantic structure of the proverb itself. Thirdly, features characterizing the proverb with regard to the surrounding context.
>
> The proverb if it is used in connection with a speech utterance, is separated from the speaking subject [speaker] by the fact that the speaking subject uses the proverb but is not in fact its originator. This desubjectivization [depersonalization] of the proverb is connected with three properties: the traditional nature of the proverb, the collective acceptance which is a necessary prerequisite for a proverb, and finally the feeling of the presence of a foreign subject [third party] who by means of the proverb is involved in the utterance.
>
> The traditional nature of the proverb, that is, a kind of lasting value which extends beyond the context of the occasion, is shared with a whole set of other forms of speech utterance. Such traditional forms are above all clichés of the most varied kind, be it fixed expressions that are mere sentence constituents, or entire sentences (such as politeness expressions). Similarly there is a traditional character also to various kinds of formulae such as those which accompany certain legal acts (for instance an oath formula, a promotion formula, etc.).

p. 294

> The difference between cliché and formula, which is not a very sharp one, incidentally, consists in the fact that the unchangeability of a formula has the nature of a command: a formula when all is said and done always has some kind of symbolic character and this symbolic value and effect is linked to the unchangeability of its wording. As far as the proverb is concerned, it oscillates between cliché and formula. If it is used authoritatively, as an instruction or something like it, it is closer to a formula; if it is used more casually as a simple part of the stream of speech it is closer to a cliché, without however coinciding with either one of the two; the proverb has some aspects which are missing in either cliché or formula--in considering any of the properties of the proverb one must keep in mind that none of these properties alone gives a full characterization of the proverb, but only the complete set of properties. In this connection one must also remember that the proverb has some points in common with those traditional semantic complexes that are known as truisms (commonplaces); a truism is not bound to a particular constantly repeated wording, on the other hand the idea which forms its core is repeated not only in its basic quality but also in the progress of its development [theme]. As a consequence a truism creates the

p. 294

> impression of being self-evident and thanks to this impression it sometimes can pretend to a degree of conviction which the underlying idea in and of itself may not have. This is of course also the case with proverbs: using a proverb sometimes the speaker can escape being under the control of realities which would be in conflict with the assertion that he has made by using a proverb. It is therefore possible that the proverb shares with the truism the traditional nature of its intellectual core and its development--without of course coinciding with the truism. The proverb is most closely similar to a truism when it is used without particular regard to its content and only for the purpose of helping the speaker out of some embarrassment,

p. 295

> if he wishes to answer indefinitely or without obligation; these same purposes are on other occasions served by a truism the underlying idea of which is by automatization deprived of all definiteness.
>
> A further characteristic of the proverb which is related to its connection with the speaking subject is collective acceptance, that is to say the acceptance of both its thought and its wording by the entire community for which a proverb is a proverb. Let us underline here that the romantic thesis which perceives the proverb as a treasure of folk wisdom is based on the existence of this collective acceptance, and that this collective acceptance connects the proverb to other forms of folk creativity.
>
> To this day a speaker in using a proverb is invoking a general consensus about the idea expressed or at least presupposed by the proverb.
>
> Both collective acceptance and traditionality are the consequences of the socialization of certain forms of expression which originally must have been individual. Collective acceptance here however, as opposed to traditionality which is passive, seems to be an active factor: something that has achieved social acceptance is not only generally used but also generally accepted as correct.

p. 296

> Functions can appear in clusters so that it isn't possible to designate any one of them as unequivocally dominant. A folk song may at the same time be also satire, exhortation, confession of love, i.e. an extra aesthetic event; and be a dance song, that is an event which to a large extent is aesthetic, and the concrete situation when the song is sung will decide which of these functions will be in the foreground.
>
> The fact that collective acceptance is necessary for all

Appendix B

p. 296

proverbs does not however mean that the folk would create all of the proverbs that it has accepted as its own--present-day research has shown quite clearly that a good many proverbs are not of folk origin but of bookish origin and that proverbs can move

p. 297

from one people to another. The collective acceptance therefore should not be judged only from the point of view of the origin of these proverbs, which incidentally is accessible only to specialists. Nor can it be judged only in the light of the extent to which a given proverb is alive in a folk environment or was alive in it. A proverb affects us as a proverb not because we would be assured ahead of time that the group has accepted it as a fixed expression of its attitude to things but on the contrary: when we hear an utterance which affects us by some of its characteristics as if it were a proverb (for instance by its formal or semantic structure), we then ascribe to this utterance the dignity that arises from collective acceptance even though further examination might show that it is an artificial sentence. Collective acceptance is therefore not so much linked to the proverb itself as linked to the attitude that the perceiver has with regard to the proverb.

A proverb which occurs as part of a speech utterance gives the speaker the impression of using a foreign expression and gives the hearer the impression that someone other than the speaker has interfered in the act of speech. The proverb is thus for both of the parties that are involved in an act of speech accompanied by the impression of the presence of a foreign subject. In this regard the proverb is by no means an isolated phenomenon; there are many elements which within a given speech event give the impression of coming from a foreign subject: the general term that is usually applied to them is quotations.

By opposition to other quotations the subjects of a proverb is felt to be a general subject--this is a consequence of its collective acceptance. We are here not particularly interested in the differences, we are interested mainly in the things that proverbs have in common with other quotations--and that is the feeling that there is a foreign subject that intrudes into the context.

p. 298

There is in the given case no reason for us not to call quotations all those components of an utterance which brings a foreign subject into it.

A quotation is an element which is highlighted against its context, it differs from it. This opposition is of course of a dialectic nature because it does not mean isolation within the context. A quotation at the same time attempts to be singled

Selected Passages from Mukařovský (1971)   101

p. 298

out in context and to merge with it. Proof of the second tendency is the existence of various shades of semi-direct and indirect speech which are so richly taken advantage of by modern epic prose.

The separation of the citation from its surrounding context is closely connected with another characteristic of the quotation, namely its free semantic relation to the connectedness of the semantic line of the context and to the factual situation on which the context is based and to which it refers.

p. 299

A quotation may often serve to indicate something that the speaker for whatever reason does not wish to say out directly; thus a quotation often may have the value of an allusion or a euphemism. Not only does the quotation have an effect on the meaning of the context but conversely, the effect of the context may give this quotation a meaning which it does not have of itself; for instance whenever it is used ironically.

As is well known the speech of educated people contains a certain store of conventionalized quotations (where very often the author isn't even generally known and which nevertheless retain their character of quotes).

There is a variety of shades of meaning of which quotes are capable.

There is a concentration of attention on the wording of a quote.

Another important characteristic of the quote is that it has a tendency to be an utterance addressed to someone that is spoken with particular attention to someone (to the hearer). This is of course not the case for each use of a quotation, thus a quotation in a scholarly work doesn't usually have even the trace of the direct reference to the hearer, but such a regard to the hearer can be quite noticeable and sometimes even dominant in quotations used

p. 300

in conversation. This arises from the fact that a quotation here may be applied as a value judgment and such a value judgment is not given by the nature of the thing itself, but given by the relation of the evaluating subject to the thing evaluated (scolding, praise, ridicule, warning); the evaluator, the speaking subject, takes a certain position to the matter at hand by virtue of the use of the quote and exhorts the listener to take that same position. Thus this 'addressed nature' of the quotation is one of the reasons why quotations are often felt as making speech 'more lively.' Even in a monologue quotations can create the impressions of a dialogue; hence the predilection that orators have for quotations since they often use quotations for the same purposes as an apostrophe,

Appendix B

p. 300

a rhetorical question, etc., that is, to bring the hearer into direct connection with the utterance.

This 'addressed nature' of quotations brings us back to the original point made, namely to the fact that a quotation allows a foreign subject to intrude into the utterance (someone else, a third person, speaks through the mouth of the speaker). This circumstance as we have already said is the most fundamental for the characterization of a quotation. The awareness that the quotation involves a duality of the speaking subject (the speaker plus the author of the quotation) serves to strengthen to a considerable extent in the hearer the feeling for the subject from whom the utterance came as well as the tension between the various subjects that take part in this utterance; that is, between the author of the citation, the speaker and the hearer. Thus a quotation can serve not only to 'dialogize' a conversation but also to theatricalize it.

These cases are however only an extreme manifestation of a tendency which, all things considered, is present in any quotation: even a scholarly quotation is not free of a strengthened feeling of the subject that stands behind the utterance and a strengthened tension between the subjects that have common authorship of a sort at the moment the quotation is being applied; this becomes particularly apparent when the author of a text takes a polemic attitude towards the author of a quotation and the reader is forced to decide whom to agree with.

p. 301

All of the different aspects and characteristics of the quotations mentioned so far can also apply in the case of the proverb, so long as the latter functions as and is perceived to be a quotation. The proverb is likewise in its context felt to be both a foreign element and a part of the context. As far as its isolation from the surrounding context is concerned, it is enough to think of the various devices--both 'formal' and semantic--used by the proverb to bring about its closure and completeness. As far as the opposite tendency is concerned, that is, the tendency to merge into the context, one must above all think of the fact that the proverb which is used as a genuinely independent entity---as an entity totally removed from the context--is no longer perceived as a proverb but as something else such as an inscription or a slogan (compare the 'Gnóthi seauton' at the entrance to the Delphic oracle). One must further be reminded of the tendency that the proverb had to further develop the image contained in it beyond its own boundaries (see about that in the introduction to this study). As far as the loose relationship of the proverb to the continuity of the semantic line is concerned, we shall see later on with much evidence clearly and apparently to what extent it is important for the proverb, and characteristic, to have a variety of shades of meaning which bring about this very loosening. It is also the case that the concentration of attention on the

p. 301

wording manifests itself very intensively in the case of the proverb. In this regard the proverb displays all the characteristics of poetic expression as well as the exceptionality and unusualness of poetic style; in addition to rhyme, alliteration, parallelism, etc., which can serve as the devices for bringing about both the semantic and the phonetic completion of the proverb, and in addition to the preference the proverbs have for imagery which also has its extraaesthetic function, we must point to the fact that proverbs often also contain unusual words, particularly archaic expressions. This tendency explains why--similarly to other kinds of quotations--in the case of proverbs one feels the necessity of 'verbatim' citation.

p. 302

In addition the proverb agrees with quotations in the respect of being used as a form of addressed speech. Even this--and this particularly expressively--is usually applied in an evaluative manner: the presence of an evaluative element is--as will be shown in more detail--one of the essential characteristics both of the proverb itself and its use. Finally, the duality of the speaking subject and the consequences that stem from it, that is, the intensive feeling of 'dialogization' or even 'theatricalization' of an utterance by the use of a quotation, can be found without any difficulty to be present in the case of proverbs as well. If proverbs are used frequently in a monologue utterance, this creates semantic twists at the border between the proverb and the surrounding context which give the context the appearance of a dialogue.

p. 303

Because a proverb is a traditional utterance backed up by the group and perceived in the process of uttering as having arisen from another subject than the speaker, because of all this a proverb is spontaneously felt to be an authoritative utterance with supra-subjective validity. By using a proverb the speaker refers, sometimes silently, sometimes overtly, to the age of this utterance, to the general recognition of its truth or obligatoriness ('it isn't in vain that we have been saying for all these years . . .' etc.). It is natural that the authoritative nature of the proverb is not always stressed in the case of use. There are cases when the proverb can serve a purpose where this authoritative quality remains entirely in the background--thus for instance when one plays with its imagistic meaning.

p. 305

The analysis of the authoritative validity of proverbs is the end of the enumeration and analysis of the first group of characteristics of the proverb, those which arise from the relation of the proverb, to the speaking subject. Now comes another sey of characteristics, namely those which have to do with the internal semantic structure of proverbs. These are the following

Appendix B

p. 305

characteristics: the generalizing meanings of proverbs; further, its norm creating and evaluative nature; finally, then, the figurativeness of the meaning of the proverb both in its parts and in its totality; . . . The final characteristic which is rooted in all of these three previous characteristics and sums them up is the fundamental ambiguity of the proverb. While the previous group of characteristics dealt with the relation of the proverb to something

p. 306

that is beyond its internal structure, that is, to the subject of the proverb in its capacity of utterance, the group of characteristics that we now wish to analyze deals with the internal structure of the proverb itself.

We shall give particular attention above all to the generalizing meaning and the evaluative nature of the proverb.

The proverb has as many different aspects as there are phenomena related to it, and as many relations to other phenomena as there are aspects to it.

p. 334

A proverb functions in a context above all as a generalizing statement.

p. 335

A proverb in its context furthermore functions as a quotation.

p. 336

And finally the third thing: a proverb functions in its context also as a cliché.

p. 339

The proverb requires a context and lives a full life only in a context. On the other hand, the proverb also stands in opposition to its context--it is isolated from it and it also shatters its semantic structure. Therefore the context in which the proverb functions most conspicuously is the context of dialogue which is full of semantic twists. Here the proverb is in its element: it reinforces these semantic twists and becomes their means of execution.

p. 340

We still haven't said in its entirety what is the basic role of the proverb in a context: it consists essentially in the fact that a proverb is in its context perceived as a synonymn which replaces a more direct expression--hence always its distance in a certain sense from the context.

APPENDIX C
FLOW CHART OF CONFLICT SEQUENCE

Flow Chart of Conflict Sequence, Part I

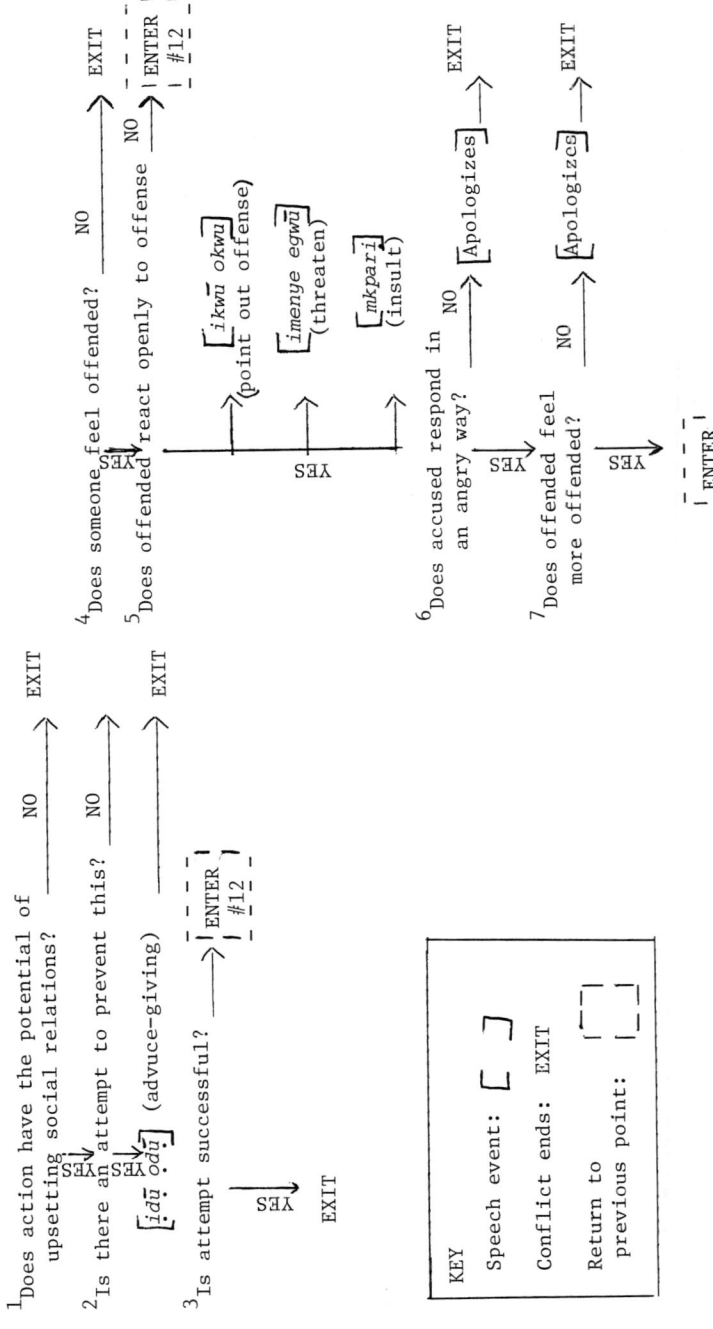

Flow Chart of Conflict Sequence, Part II

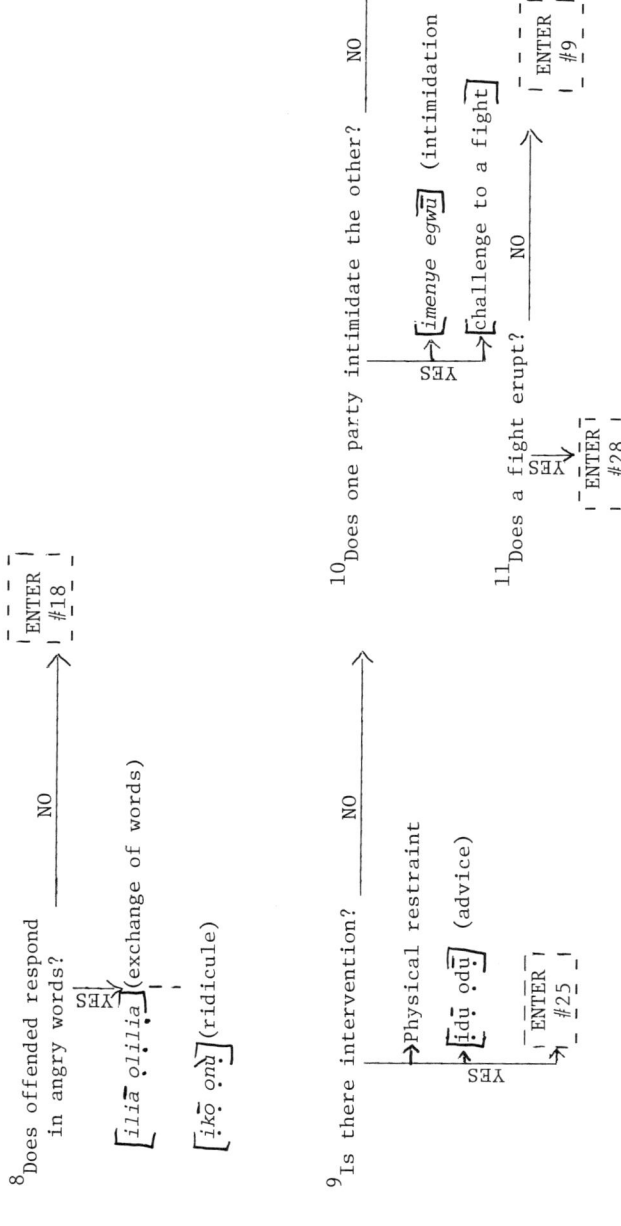

Flow Chart of Conflict Sequence, Part III

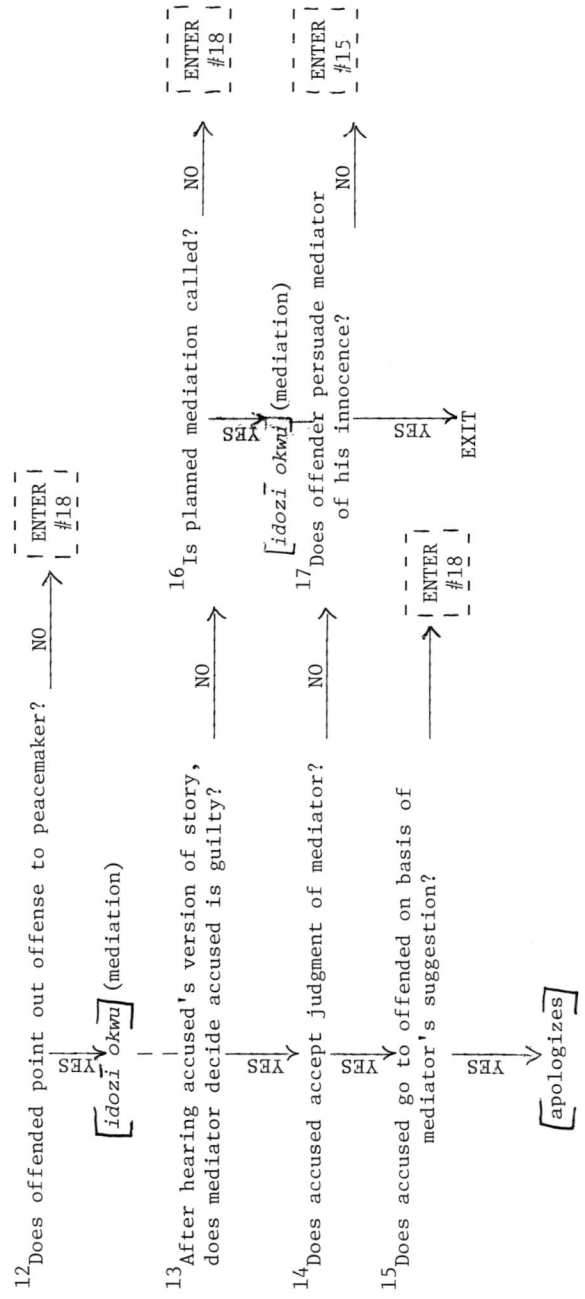

Flow Chart of Conflict Sequence, Part IV

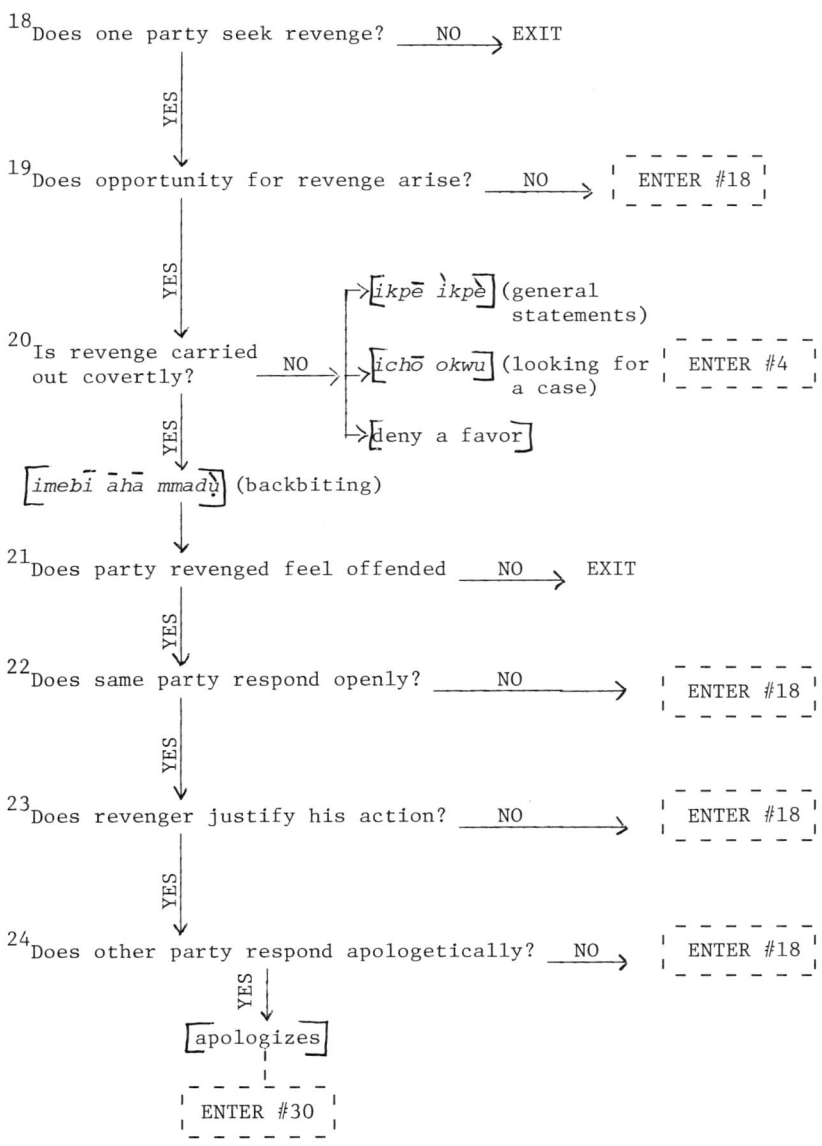

Flow Chart of Conflict Sequence, Part V

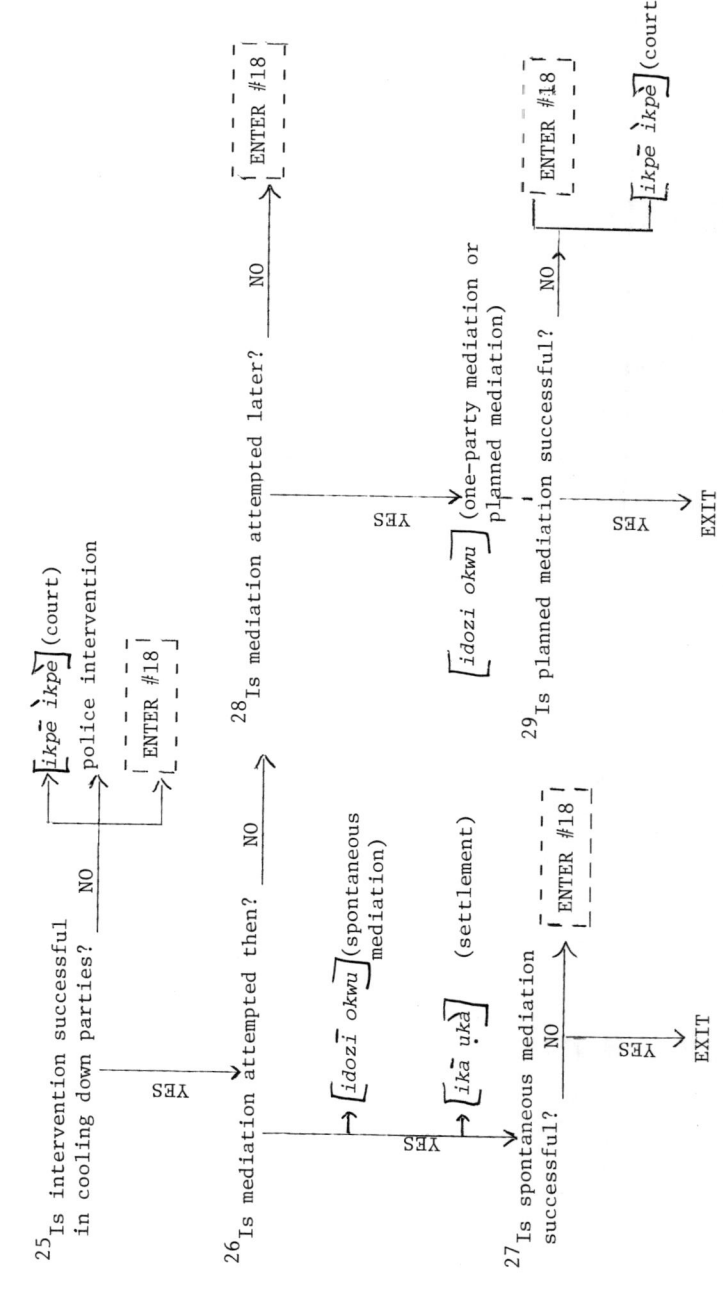

APPENDIX D
REFERENCE LIST OF PROVERBS

This list includes only those Igbo proverbs to which reference is made in the text of this study. They are listed according to the order in which they were collected by the researcher.

1. A nà èle ofe nwanyì n'ǫnū.

    L.T. By tasting a woman's soup with your mouth, you prove how good it is.

    P.T. The taste of the pudding is in the eating.

2, Wère irē gī gùǫ ezē gī ǫnū.

    L.T. Use your tongue to count your teeth.

    P.T. Think more and you will find the answer.

3. Ọ̀kukò mmanya nà-ègbu, à hùbeghī ufù ara na-awì.

    L.T. A chicken who is drunk has never seen a fox who is mad.

    P.T. When a person who feels he is very strong meets with someone who is stronger, then he knows his dilemma.

4. Òjì ǫsǫ àghakwū ọ̀gụ̀, amaghī nà ọ̀gụ̀ bụ̀ ǫnwụ̄ njǫ.

    L.T. One who rushes to a fight doesn't know that fighting is dangerous.

    P.T. Those who look for trouble might not be aware of the consequences involved.

5. *Agha a kàrà àkà àdighī, èri onye ngwǭrǭ.*

    L.T. A planned war doesn't take the life of a cripple.

    P.T. To be forewarned is to be forearmed.

6. *Nkịta nà ewū ànaghī ēgwū egwū.*

    L.T. Dog and goat shouldn't play together.

    P.T. People or animals of the same sex or species are supposed to cling together.

7. *Egbe bère ùgò bère, ǹkè sī ihe yā, ēbēlà ǹkwù kwāā yā.*

    L.T. Hawk and eagle perched on a tree. If the hawk does not allow the eagle to perch, his wing should break off.

    P.T. To cheat another is bad. (Live and let live.)

8. *À dighī ārāpù isi aka, àgba ụfụụ.*

    L.T. You can't snap your fingers without your thumb.

    P.T. Certain functions have to be performed by certain people.

9. *À naghī èji ihe à nà-àgba na ntị àgba n'anya.*

    L.T. You shouldn't use a thing for cleaning the ears to clean the eyes.

    P.T. Use things for the purpose fow which they were intended.

10. *Ebe ọ sọ̀rọ̀ nwanyị̀ yā kpụ̀a arā, ọ gà-ènyenata.*

    L.T. Let a female develop her breast, eventually she must give it to her child.

    P.T. Remember that a female is supposed to act like a female.

11. *Chọ̀wa akwà gị̄ ebe i sàrà àhụ.*

    L.T. Start looking for your cloth where you took your bath.

    P.T. Direct your attention to the appropriate place.

12. *Mbè sị̀ nà ozu ọ̀zọ gà-ànwụ*

    L.T. Tortoise said another death will occur.

    P.T. Your need will occur again.

13. *Okokpòrò jụ́rụ́ ikpòfu ntụ ụtụ́tụ́.*

    L.T. Bachelors refuse to remove their ashes [from the fire] in the morning.

    P.T. You can't avoid your responsibilities forever.

14. Ọ̀bịalụ̀ èle m̄ ọ̄mụ̄gwò. gwàrà ǹdị̀ ọ̀zọ màkà ọrụ nwanyị̀.

   L.T. She who came to take care of the new mother during the time of after-birth gave out information [to others] about the new mother's vagina.

   P.T. When one was to perform certain duties, they started releasing additional information not part of their original duty to others.

15. I kwē onye ikpèchị̀ n'aka, ibị̀ ọmà àguwa yā.

   L.T. If you shake hands with someone with yaws, he will desire to embrace you.

   P.T. Give someone an inch and they take a mile.

16. Wepụ̀ akā ēnwē n'ofē, nà ọ̀ dị̀ kà akā mmādụ̀.

   L.T. Remove the hand of a monkey from the stew or else it looks like the hand of a human.

   P.T. An ounce of prevention is worth a pound of cure.

17. Otu nwanyị̀ gbatara kà ọ̀ nà-èzi di ya.

   L.T. It is the woman's private parts [sexual parts] that are shown to the husband.

   P.T. Whatever one has is what they show to those close to them.

18. Ùgo ọ̀kụkọ̀ nwèrè bù abụ̄hā ya.

   L.T. The dignity of a fowl is its feathers.

   P.T. There is a person who stands as the pillar of the family or group of people.

19. Agbisi gbāā òtele, ya amụ̄rụ̄ àkọ.

   L.T. If ants bite one's anus, one learns a lesson.

   P.T. Once harmed, you learn a lesson.

20. Chi jie, anya mà ènyị̀ ya.

   L.T. When darkness comes, the eye knows its friend.

   P.T. No matter how bad conditions may be, friends recognize each other.

21. Nwanyị jị ụkwụ ya gata ihe, ya sị na ụmụ di ya nyèrè ya.

   L.T. When a woman gets gifts by prostitution, she says her husband's relatives gave them to her.

   P.T. When a person gets things illicitly, they tend to give unsound reasons to support their claim.

22. Agadi nwanyi dàa n'àlà ugbòrò, àbùa, à gùa ihe di n'àbọ ya ọnu.

   L.T. When an old woman falls twice, people begin to count the things in her basket.

   P.T. Two failures and people will hold you responsible or begin to suspect your ability.

23. Onye àfụ ọnu adighi àfụ ọkụ.

   L.T. A man with a beard shouldn't blow on fire.

   P.T. People with certain restrictions should take the necessary precautions.

24. Òri nkè mmàdù, mmàdù ò nà-èrikwa nke ya?

   L.T. He who eats others' things, when will others eat his own?

   P.T. Those who enjoy the generosity of others should also give something in return.

25. Ọkụkọ tujụọ àlà, olu agọọ ya.

   L.T. If a chicken pecks and misses, his neck gets twisted.

   P.T. If you do something wrong to someone, the gods will punish you.

26. Kamà mgba jì-apụ ọgụ, kà mmiri zọọ.

   L.T. Instead of wrestling turn into fighting, let the rain fall.

   P.T. Prevention of trouble is better than cure.

27. Ebe àlà di nsó anaghi èshi àgùgọ mgba.

   L.T. When the ground is near, arguing about wrestling [who will defeat whom] is futile.

   P.T. When you have the means to prove something, use the means instead of postponing it.

28. Òke sòrò ngwèrè màa mmiri, mmiri kọọ ngwere, ọ gaghi akọ oke.

   L.T. If a rat follows the lizard into the rain, they both get get drenched but the water dries off the lizard while it doesn't dry off the rat.

   P.T. People shouldn't follow those who are in different social positions than themselves.

29. Mpàkọ nri bùtèrè, ònye sìri nkè a.

   L.T. When people gather food together, it brings up the question who cooked this.

   P.T. Familiarity breeds contempt.

30. *Onye tàa m̄ arụ̄ ńikè asọghī ǹsi m̄ tàa, ya n'isi àgaghì m̄ àsọ ụbụ̀rụ.*

   L.T. If a thing that bites you in the anus is not deterred by your feces, when you bite it you will not consider its brain.

   P.T. If a person harms you without consideration of your relationship, when you revenge you do so without consideration of him.

31. *Ọ̀kukọ̀ ụkwù jìrì, à nāghī èrè ya nà dìàlà.*

   L.T. You shouldn't sell a chicken with a bad leg to a free-born.

   P.T. You don't cheat a friend.

32. *Kà ahā èri, anāghī èri ibe ha.*

   L.T. Those who eat together, shouldn't eat each other.

   P.T. Friends shouldn't maltreat friends.

33. *Ọ̀kukọ̀ hapùrù onye gbùrù yā, mà tùgobarọ ìtè olu.*

   L.T. The chicken left the person who killed it and tooks its anger out on the pot.

   P.T. Blame is often misplaced.

34. *Ogbū agwọ nà-àchọ ndù, agwọ ọ̀ nà-ègbu nà-àchọkwa ǹkè ya.*

   L.T. A person trying to kill a snake should remember that the snake also wants to live.

   P.T. When you try to harm someone, remember he will be trying to harm you too.

35. *Onye pụtara ùra ụtụ̀tù, ọ̀kukọ̀ chụ̀wa ya ọsọ, ya gbàwa n'ìhī nà ọ̀ maghī mà o pùru èzē n'àbàlì.*

   L.T. He who wakes in the morning and is chased by a chicken should run away because he doesn't know whether the chicken grew teeth during the night.

   P.T. When someone behaves in a peculiar way, you shouldn't stay to argue with him.

36. *Nnụ̀nù fèe ajọ ùfe, à gbanyere ya ājō ākụ̀.*

   L.T. A swift bird requires a swift bow to catch it.

   P.T. Sudden happenings need to be treated promptly.

37. *Mmadụ̀ àdighị̀ àma ṁgbè ọ gàfèrè n'ama ibe ọgọ̀ ya.*

   L.T. A person doesn't know when he crosses through his in-law's compound.

P.T. Treat everyone nice because you don't know who you might be mistreating and how they might be related to you in the future.

38. *Onye è jedòrò n'ùkwù òsè, ghọrọ osè.*

    L.T. A person caught in a pepper garden is accused of stealing peppers.

    P.T. If you go where you shouldn't, you can be termed guilty of an offense.

39. *Onye gotere egbè ọhuru nà-èje ụlọ akwa onye toro afọ.*

    L.T. A person with a new gun shoots it at a funeral at which the shooting of guns is forbidden.

    P.T. Power intoxicates.

40. *Nwatà gotere àkpà ohụ̀rụ̀ nà-ànya ya wèrè àlabà ụrā.*

    L.T. A child who gets a new bag loves it so much he sleeps with it.

    P.T. When a person finally gets what he has sought for a long time, he tends to overuse it.

41. *A dàa elu à hụ̀ọ àlà mmā.*

    L.T. When a person falls, he becomes acquainted with the nature of the ground.

    P.T. One learns from his mistakes.

42. *A ghaa àkụ ọ̀ tụ n'ogwe, a ghaa àkụ ọ̀ tụ n'ogwe, ọ̀ bụ̀ ogwè kà a pịịrị̀ àkụ?*

    L.T. You shoot an arrow, it hits a log; you shoot a second arrow, it hits the same log; is it this log the arrow is meant for?

    P.T. A person who is frequently involved in disputes has few chances of establishing his innocence.

43. *Aka nrī kwōọ aka èkpè, aka èkpè àkwōọ aka nrī.*

    L.T. The right hand washes the left hand, the left hand washes the right hand.

    P.T. One should repay those who show them kindness by showing them kindness in return. Or help one another.

44. *Onye nà-àchụ okụkọ̀ nwē ada, nwā okụkọ̀ nwē ọsọ.*

    L.T. He who pursues a chicken will fall while the chicken runs free.

Reference List of Proverbs 117

     P.T.   A person trying to harm an innocent person is often harmed himself.

45. *E memaa onye akịdị ya ebute ọzọ.*

     L.T.   If you treat a person who brings you beans in a nice way, he will bring more.

     P.T.   If you show appreciation to one who does you a favor, he will do more.

46. *Onye buru ukwà mụo àgha anya n'àzụ, ọ bughī ogè ọ nà-àchutā ya.*

     L.T.   One who carries the breadfruit of a spirit looks behind him while running away.

     P.T.   A clear conscience fears nothing.

47. *Ihe ọma m egbulà m.*

     L.T.   Let my kindness never kill me.

     P.T.   Let others reward me for my good deeds.

48. *E bìri egò kwụọ ụgwọ, ụgwọ dịkwà ebe ọ dị.*

     L.T.   A debtor who borrows to pay his debt is still a debtor.

     P.T.   You can't rob Peter to pay Paul.

49. *A chọwa ihe à nà-àgwa nwa dī mma àsi ya kùrù mmiri sachaa àhụ.*

     L.T.   If you can't insult a beautiful person, you tell him to go take a bath.

     P.T.   When you can't find a major fault in someone, you search for trivial ones.

50. *Nwatā gbere igbe tụọ mụ mbo, mụ egbere igbe ga tụgwara, à naghī àma àma o nwēe ihe àlà zirì ya.*

     L.T.   If a child crawls and scratches you, you should crawl and scratch him in return, because you don't know who told him to scratch you.

     P.T.   People can do wrong to you as a result of advice given to them.

51. *Dupū m bụ urè, ò nweghī onye agaghī àlarụ.*

     L.T.   You escort another for the joy of it not because he won't reach home.

     P.T.   A person can manage to do things for himself if others are not willing to cheerfully help him.

52. *Ezi ụzọ azụ ulọ, mà àlughìrì ya ọgụ ọ naghī echi.*

     L.T.   Path-making behind one's house continues until there is

Appendix D

   a fight.
   P.T. People act very aggressively when pursuing their rights.

53. Onye nkirika akwa, anaghī àga ebe à nà-àbu ògù.

   L.T. A person with tattered clothes shouldn't go to a place where there is fighting.
   P.T. A person with very little is cautious not to lose it.

54. Ehi enweghī odù, chi ya nà-àchuru ya ijiji.

   L.T. If a cow has no tail, God helps him to drive away the flies.
   P.T. Helpless people receive help through providence.

55. Nkumè dì mma inyà n'ólu mà ọ bụ̀ ònye mkpọkpụ ya?

   L.T. Some stones are pretty when worn as necklaces but who is going to bore the hole in them?
   P.T. The idea is good but carrying it out is difficult.

56. Oji oso agbakwuru ògu, amaghi na ògu bu onwu.

   L.T. A person who rushes to war doesn't know he may meet death.
   P.T. If you rush into things without thinking, it's likely you will be harmed.

57. A naghī ègbu atụrụ màkà olu ya di ogologo.

   L.T. You shouldn't kill a sheep because it has a long neck.
   P.T. Don't take advantage of someone because they are weak.

58. Òchìcha biàgòdù nà pūkū otu nwà ọ̀kụkọ̀ gà-àtụtụrụchā ha.

   L.T. Even if cockroaches come in thousands, one chicken can clear them all.
   P.T. An intelligent person can defeat a thousand fools.

59. Ọ̀gba oso anaghī àgba ghàrà ihụ̄ àlà.

   L.T. Wherever you run, there is nowhere you don't touch the ground.
   P.T. The ancestors and the sacred ground [Ala] know whatever you do.

60. Ụkà bù nkà.

   L.T. Speech is an art.
   P.T. Those who don't know the art of speaking are often misunderstood and embarrassed.

Reference List of Proverbs 119

61. *Nwanyì ólu ọma, di anaghī̀ àjụrụ ya nrī.*

    L.T. The food of a woman who speaks sweetly is never rejected by her husband.

    P.T. One good turn deserves another. Politeness is often rewarded with politeness.

62. *Mmiri machie anụ ukwu ọkpà, ọ̀ naghī̀ àmachi ihe e kwùrù n'ọnū.*

    L.T. Water may cover the footprint on the ground but it does not cover the words of the mouth.

    P.T. Abusive words spoken are not easily forgotten.

63. *Ire di n'ọnū̀ ji ǹkà anyā ezē.*

    L.T. The tongue survives the teeth through carefulness.

    P.T. A skillful use of strategies helps one to survive.

64. *Okwu di njọ na ntì adighī̀ mmā.*

    L.T. No unpleasant word is liked by the ear.

    P.T. No one likes to be insulted.

65. *Onye ogọ nne mmadù̀ nà-èmè kà agọwa nne ya.*

    L.T. He who curses another's mother is asking that his own mother be cursed.

    P.T. He who harms a person is asking to be harmed in return.

66. *Nwata kwùe okwù, à màrà kà àhụ ya ra.*

    L.T. When a child speaks, his maturity is portrayed.

    P.T. You know someone's intelligence by his actions.

67. *A tụ̀rụ̀ ilu kà ọ̀ gbà onyē ǹzūzū ghārị̀ị̀.*

    L.T. Proverbs are used to confuse stupid people.

    P.T. Only those who are knowledgeable in proverbs are able to understand them when they are used.

68. *Ụkà a kàrà m̀gbe adi mma, m̀gbe aderi njo, akpa ya isi.*

    L.T. When there is mutual conversation, things are fine; when there is no longer peace a dispute comes up.

    P.T. When things go peacefully, everything is fine but when things go contrary and people fall out with one another then lies come in.

69. *Èri ekwē mèrè nwanyì aghalā afụ̄ ọnụ̄.*

L.T. Eating and denying was the cause for women to not have whiskers.

P.T. Honesty is the best policy.

70. Otù nwoke sị onye gwàrà ya okwu nà ọtọ̀rọ̀ ya, ya agwa ya okwù onye tọrọ ya gwàrà ya.

L.T. A man once said if a person tells him something and claims that it was told to him by his senior, he would quote something from someone who seniored that man.

P.T. There is always someone who knows a lot as to challenge one's credibility.

71. Onye nà-àkpo nkịta òkù jìre apịpia n'àkà, ọ̀ sị̀ ya bịa kà ọ̀ sị̀ ya abịalà?

L.T. He who calls a dog and carries a stick in his hand, does he want the dog to come or not to come?

P.T. Saying one thing and doing another hurts others.

72. E jì ụkà ème ụkà.

L.T. You use speech in making a speech.

P.T. Quote past events for present circumstances.

BIBLIOGRAPHY

Abel, R. L. 1973. "A Comparative Theory of Dispute Institutions in Society," Law and Society, Winter: 217-348.

Abrahams, R. D. 1962. "Playing the Dozens," Journal of American Folklore, 75:209-220.

_____. 1968. "Introductory Remarks to a Rhetorical Theory of Folklore," Journal of American Folklore, 81:143-158.

_____. 1972. "Proverbs and Proverbial Expressions," in R. Dorson, ed., Folklore and Folklife: An Introduction. Chicago: University of Chicago Press, 117-127.

_____. 1974. "Black Talking on the Streets," in R. Bauman and J. Sherzer, eds., Explorations in the Ethnography of Speaking. New York: Cambridge University Press, 240-262.

Achebe, C. 1958. Things Fall Apart. London: Heinemann.

_____. 1964. Arrow of God. Garden City, N.Y.: Doubleday and Company, Inc.

Africa Research Bulletin, 1974. April 15-May 14: 3104.

Albert, E. M. 1972. "'Rhetoric,' 'Logic,' and 'Poetics' in Burundi: Culture Patterning of Speech Behavior," in J. Gumperz and D. Hymes, eds., Directions in Sociolinguistics: The Ethnography of Communication. New York: Holt, Rinehart, and Winston, 33-56.

Bibliography

Arewa, E. O. 1970. "Proverb Usage in 'Natural' Context and Oral Literary Criticism," Journal of American Folklore, 83:430-437.

_____ and A. Dundes. 1964. "Proverbs and the Ethnography of Speaking Folklore," in J. Gumperz and D. Hymes, eds., The Ethnography of Communication. American Anthropological Association Special Publication, 66, (6), Part 2.

Asongwed, T. 1975. "The Novelist as a Naive Ethnologist: A Study of Code-Switching." Paper presented at 1975 Conferences on Culture and Communication, Temple University, Philadelphia, March 13-15.

Austin, J. L. 1962. How to Do Things with Words. ed. by J. O. Urmson. New York: Oxford University Press.

Barth, F. 1966. Models of Social Organization. Royal Anthropological Institute. Occasional Paper No. 23. London: Royal Anthropological Institute.

Bascom, W. R. 1955. "Verbal Art," Journal of American Folklore, 68:245-252.

_____. 1965. "Folklore and Literature," in R. A. Lystad, ed., The African World: A Survey of Social Research. New York: Frederick Praeger.

Basden, G. T. 1921. Among the Ibos of Southern Nigeria. London: London: Seeley Service.

Basso, K. and H. Selby, eds. 1976. Meaning in Anthropology. New Mexico: University of New Mexico Press.

Bauman, R. 1977. "Linguistics, Anthropology, and Verbal Art: Toward a Unified Perspective with a Special Discussion of Children's Folklore." Paper presented at the 28th Annual Georgetown University Round Table on Languages and Linguistics, Washington, D.C., 1977.

_____ and J. Sherzer, eds. 1974. Explorations in the Ethnography of Speaking. New York: Cambridge University Press.

_____. 1975. "The Ethnography of Speaking," in B. Siegel, A. Beals, and S. Tyler, eds., Annual Review of Anthropology, Vol. 4. Palo Alto, California: Annual Reviews, Inc., 95-119.

Benedict, R. 1934. Patterns of Culture. Cambridge, Mass.: Riverside Press.

Bennett, J. W. and H. M. Tumin. 1964. "Some Cultural Imperatives," in P. Hammond, ed., Cultural and Social Anthropology. London: Collier-Macmillan Limited, 9-22.

Bergsma, H. M. 1970. "Tiv Proverbs as a Means of Social Control," *Africa*, 40: 151-153.

Bird, C. and T. Shopen. n.d. *Maninka*. Center for Applied Linguistics. Mimeo.

Bohannan, P. 1963. *Social Anthropology*. New York: Holt, Rinehart, and Winston.

Botkin, B. A. 1962. "The Folkness of the Folk," in H. Beck, ed., *Folklore in Action*. Philadelphia: The American Folklore Society, 44-57.

Bradbury, R. E. 1957. *The Benin Kingdom and the Edo-Speaking Peoples of South-Western Nigeria*. London: International African Institute.

Brown, I. C. 1963. *Understanding Other Cultures*. Englewood Cliffs, N.J." Prentice-Hall, Inc.

Carnochan, J. and B. Iwuchuku. 1963. *An Igbo Revision Course*. London: Oxford University Press.

Christensen, J. B. 1958. "The Role of Proverbs in Fante Culture," *Africa*, 28: 232-243.

Chuwukere, B. I. 1971. "Individualism: An Aspect of Igbo Religion," *The Conch*, 3, 2: 109-117.

Cicourel, A. 1972. "Basic and Normative Rules in the Negotiation of Status and Role," in D. Sudnow, ed., *Studies in Social Interaction*. New York: The Free Press, 229-258.

Clifton, J., ed. 1967. *Introduction to Cultural Anthropology*. Boston: Houghton Mifflin.

Daniel, Jack. 1972. "Towards an Ethnography of Afroamerican Proverbial Usage, *Black Lines*.

Dorson, R., ed. 1972. *Folklore and Folklife: An Introduction*. Chicago: University of Chicago Press.

Drewal, H. J. 1974. "Efe: Voiced Power and Pageantry," *African Arts*, 7, 2: 26-29, 58-66, 82-83.

Dundes, A. 1967. "Oral Literature," in J. Clifton, ed., Introduction to Cultural Anthropology. Boston: Houghton Mifflin

_____, J. W. Leach, and B. Ozkok. 1972. "The Strategy of Turkish Boys' Verbal Dueling Rhymes," in J. Gumperz and D. Hymes, eds., *Directions in Sociolinguistics: The Ethnography of Communication*. New York: Holt, Rinehart, and Winston, 130-160.

Duru, Mary. 1981. "Socialization Among the Igbo: Intergenerational

Study of Cultural Patterns, Familial Roles, and Child Rearing Patterns," Unpublished dissertation. University of Maryland.

Echeruo, M. J. C. 1971. "Igbo Thought Through Igbo Proverbs: A Comment," *The Conch*, 3, 2: 63-66.

Egudu, R. N. 1973. "Igbo Traditional Poetry and Family Relationships," *African Studies*, 32: 15-24.

Emenanjo, E. N. 1971. "Central Igbo--An Objective Appraisal." Paper presented at the Seminar on the Problems of Igbo Language and Literature, University of Nigeria, Nsukka.

_____. 1972. "Some Notes on the Use of Repetition and Contrast in Igbo Proverbs," *Ikenga*, 1, k: 109-114.

Evans-Pritchard, E. E. 1940. *The Nuer*. Oxford: Clarendon Press.

_____. 1963. *Essays in Social Anthropology*. New York: The Free Press of Glencoe, Inc.

_____. 1976. *Witchcraft, Oracles and Magic Among the Azande*. Oxford: Clarendon Press.

Farb, P. 1973. *Word Play*. New York: Bantam Books.

Finnegan, R. 1970. *Oral Literature in Africa*. Oxford: Clarendon Press.

Fishman, J. 1972. *Sociolinguistics*. Rowley, Mass." Newbury House Publishers.

Forde, C. D. 1951. *Marriage and the Family Among the Yako in South-eastern Nigeria*. London: International African Institute.

_____. 1954. *African Worlds: Studies in the Cosmological Ideas and Social Values of African Peoples*. London: Oxford University Press.

_____, and R. Scott. 1946. *The Native Economies of Nigeria*. London: Faber and Faber.

_____, and G. I. Jones. 1950. *The Ibo and Ibibio-Speaking Peoples of South-Eastern Nigeria*. (International African Institute, Ethnographic Survey of Africa, Part III). London: International African Institute.

Frake, C. O. 1972a. "How to Ask for a Drink in Subanun," in P. Giglioli, ed., *Language and Social Context*. Baltimore: Penguin Books, 87-94.

_____. 1972b. "'Struck by Speech': The Yakan Concept of Litigation," in J. Gumperz and D. Hymes, eds., *Directions in Sociolinguistics: The Ethnography of Communication*. New York: Holt, Rinehart, and Winston, 106-129.

Garvin, P. L. n.d. "The Structural Properties of Language." Mimeo.

———. 1963. "An Appraisal of Linguistics in Czechoslovakia," in T. Sebeok, ed., Current Trends in Soviet and East European Linguistics. Vol. I. The Hague: Mouton.

———. 1965. "Computer Processing and Cultural Data: Problems of Method," in D. Hymes, ed., The Use of Computers in Anthropology. The Hague: Mouton.

———. 1966. "Karl Bühler's Contribution to the Field of Linguistics," Journal of General Psychology, 75: 212-215.

———. 1977. "Functional Empiricism--An Epistemology for the Behavioral Sciences." Mimeo.

———. 1978 "An Empiricist Epistemology for Linguistics," Michel Paradis, ed., in The Fourth LACUS Forum, Montreal, 1977. Columbia, South Carolina: Hornbeam Press, Inc.

Giglioli, P. 1972. Language and Social Context. Baltimore, Maryland: Penguin Books.

Gladwin, C. 1975. "A Model of the Supply of Smoked Fish from Cape Coast to Kumasi," in S. Plattner, ed., Formal Methods in Economic Anthropology, American Anthropological Association, Special Publication, 4: 77-127.

———. 1976. "A View of the Plan Puebla: An Application of Hierarchical Decision Models," to appear in American Journal of Agriculture Economics, Proceedings, December, 1976.

Goodenough, W. H. 1965. "Rethinking 'Status' and 'Role': Toward a General Model of the Cultural Organization of Social Relationships," in M. Banton, ed., The Relevance of Models for Social Anthropology. New York: Praeger, 1-22.

Green, M. M. 1947. The Village Affairs. New York: Praeger University Series.

Greenhouse, C. J. 1976. "Non-Legal Arguments." Paper presented at the annual meeting of the American Anthropological Association, Washington, D.C., Nov. 20, 1976.

Gulliver, P. H. 1965. "Anthropology," in R. A. Lystad, ed., The African World: A Survey of Social Research. New York: Frederick Praeger, 57-106.

Gumperz, J. 1964. "Linguistic and Social Interaction in Two Communities," in J. Gumperz and D. Hymes, eds., The Ethnography of Communication. American Anthropological Association Special Publication, 66 (6), part 2.

———, and D. Hymes, eds., 1972. Directions in Socio-Linguistics: The Ethnography of Communication. New York: Holt, Rinehart,

Bibliography

and Winston.

Herskovits, M. J. 1930. "Kru Proverbs," Journal of American Folklore, 43: 225-293.

_____. 1950. "The Hypothetical Situation: A Technique of Field Research," Southwestern Journal of Anthropology, 7: 32-40.

Herzog, G. 1936. Jabo Proverbs from Liberia. London: Oxford University Press.

Hoebel, E. A. 1954. The Law of Primitive Man: A Study in Comparative Legal Dynamics. Cambridge: Harvard University Press.

Hymes, D. 1964. "Introduction: Toward Ethnographies of Communication," in J. Gumperz and D. Hymes, eds., The Ethnography of Communication. American Anthropological Association Special Publication, 66 (6), Part 2.

_____. 1965. "Review of Austin's How to Do Things with Words," American Anthropologist, 67: 587-588.

_____. 1967. "Models of the Interaction of Language and Social Setting," Journal of Social Issues, 23, 2:8-28.

_____. 1968. "The Ethnography of Speaking," in J. A. Fishman, ed., Readings in the Sociology of Language. The Hague: Mouton.

_____. 1972. "Models of the Interaction of Language and Social Life," in J. Gumperz and D. Hymes, eds., Directions in Sociolinguistics: The Ethnography of Communication. New York: Holt, Rinehart, and Winston, 35-71.

Irvine, J. T. 1974. "Strategies of Status Manipulation in the Wolof Greeting," in R. Bauman and J. Sherzer, eds., Explorations in the Ethnography of Speaking. New York: Cambridge University Press, 163-166.

Jackson, R., ed. 1966. Folklore and Society: Essays in Honor of Benjamin A. Botkin. Pennsylvania: Folklore Associates.

Keesing, R. M. 1975. Kin Groups and Social Structure. New York: Holt, Rinehart, and Winston.

Kluckhohn, C. 1949. "The Philosophy of the Navaho Indians," in F. S. C. Northrop, ed., Ideological Differences and World Order: Studies in the Philosophy and Science in the World's Cultures. New Haven: Yale University Press, 356-384.

_____, and A. L. Kroeber. 1952. "Culture: A Critical Review of Concepts and Definitions," Papers of the Peabody Museum of American Archeology and Ethnology, Harvard University.

Kochman, T. 1969. "Toward an Ethnography of Black American Speech Behavior," Trans-Action, 6: 26-34.

Krappe, A. H. 1930. *The Science of Folk-lore*. New York: Barnes and Noble.

Ladefoged, P. 1964. *A Phonetic Study of West African Languages*. West African Language Monographs, No. 1. Cambridge: The University Press.

Latis, M. 1960. "Vernacular Culture," *American Anthropologist*, 62: 202-216.

Lystad, R. A., ed. 1965. *The African World: A Survey of Social Research*. New York: Frederich Praeger.

Madubuike, I. 1974. *Structure and Meaning in Igbo Names*. State University of New York at Buffalo: Council on International Studies.

Malinowski, B. 1931. "Culture," *Encyclopedia of the Social Sciences*, 4: 621-646.

———. 1944. *A Scientific Theory of Culture and Other Essays*. Chapel Hill: The University of North Carolina Press.

Mandelbaum, D. G. 1969. "Social Groupings," in P. Hammond, ed., *Cultural and Social Anthropology*. London: Collier-Macmillan Limited, 146-162.

Mathiot, M. 1967. "The place of the Dictionary in Linguistic Description," *Language*, 43: 703-724.

———. 1970. "Theory-Building in the Descriptive Approach," in P. L. Garvin, ed., *Method and Theory in Linguistics*. The Hague: Mouton, 159-172.

———. 1973a. "Grammatical Problems in Lexicography: Grammatical Versus Lexical Status," *Annals of the New York Academy of Sciences*, 211: 39-44.

———. 1973b. "Review: La Lexicographie, ed. by Josette Rey-Debove," *Language*, 49: 961-967.

———. 1976. "On Building a Frame of Reference for the Analysis of Face-to-Face Interaction." Paper presented at the annual meeting of the American Anthropological Association, Washington, D.C., November 1976.

———, and P. L. Garvin, 1975. "The Functions of Language: A Socio-Cultural View," *Anthropological Quarterly*, 48: 148-156.

Meek, C. K. 1937. *Law and Authority in a Nigerian Tribe*. London: Oxford University Press.

Mendelson, E. M. 1968. "World View," *International Encyclopedia of the Social Sciences*, 16: 576-579.

Bibliography

Messenger, J. C., Jr. 1959. "The Role of Proverbs in a Nigerian Judicial System," Southwestern Journal of Anthropology, 15: 64-73.

_____. 1960. "Anang Proverb-Riddles," Journal of American Folklore, 73: 225-235.

Middleton, J. 1966. "The Resolution of Conflict among the Lugbara of Uganda," in M. Swartz, V. Turner and A. Tuden, eds., Political Anthropology. Chicago: Aldine, 141-154.

_____. 1968. Studies in Social and Cultural Anthropology. New York: Thomas Crowell Co.

_____, and E. H. Winter, eds., 1963. Witchcraft and Sorcery in East Africa. New York: Frederick A. Praeger.

Mitchell-Kernan, C. 1972. "Signifying and Marking: Two Afro-American Speech Acts," in J. Gumperz and D. Hymes, eds., Directions in Sociolinguistics: The Ethnography of Communication. New York: Holt, Rinehart, and Winston, 161-179.

Mukařovský, Jan. 1970. Aesthetic Function, Norm and Value as Social Facts. Michigan Slavic Contributions 3. Ann Arbor: Department of Slavics, University of Michigan.

_____. 1971. 'Prislovi jako soucast kontextu' (The proverb as a part of context). (1942-43) in Cestami poetiky a estetiky (On the track of poetics and aesthetics). Prague: Ceskoslovenský spisovatel, pp. 277-259. (Translation by Paul Garvin, personal communication).

_____. 1977. The Word and Verbal Art. Translated by John Burbank and Peter Steiner. Yale Russian and East European Studies 13. New Haven: Yale University Press.

_____. 1978. Structure, Sign and Function. Translated by John Burbank and Peter Steiner. Yale Russian and East European Studies 14. New Haven: Yale University Press, 1978.

Murdock, G. P. 1959. Africa: Its People and Their Culture History. New York: McGraw-Hill Co.

Nadel, S. F. 1954. "Morality and Language Among the Nupe," Man, 54: 55-57.

Nance, C. 1971. "Cosmology in the Novels of Chinua Achebe," The Conch, 3, 2: 121-136.

Needham, R. 1962. Structure and Sentiment: A Test Case in Social Anthropology. Chicago: University of Chicago Press.

Newman, S. 1955. "Zuni Sacred and Slang Usage," Southwestern Journal of Anthropology, oo: 345-354.

Nwoga, D. I. 1971. "The 'Chi' Individualism and Igbo Religion: A Comment," The Conch, 3,2: 30-45.

_____. 1975. "Appraisal of Igbo Proverbs and Idioms," in F. C. Ogbalu and E. N. Emenanjo, eds., Igbo Language and Culture. Oxford University Press, 186-204.

Ogbalu, F. C. 1965. Ilu Igbo. Onitsha, Nigeria: Varsity Press.

_____. n.d. Igbo Etiquette. Onitsha, Nigeria: University Publishing Co.

_____. 1974. Standard Igbo: Path to Its Development. Onitsha, Nigeria: University Publishing Co.

Okezie, J. 1977. "Quoting Behavior as Manifested in the Use of Proverbs in Igbo Society," Ph.D. dissertation, State University of New York at Buffalo. (See Penfield.)

Olisa, M. S. O. 1971. "Political Culture and Stability in Igbo Society," The Conch, 3, 2: 16-29.

Opler, Morris E. 1945. "Themes as Dynamic Forces in Culture," The American Journal of Sociology, 513: 198-206.

_____. 1959. "The Context of Themes," American Anthropologist, 51: 323-325.

Ottenberg, S. 1968. Double Descent in an African Society: The Afikpo Village-Group. Seattle: University of Washington Press.

_____. 1971. Leadership and Authority in an African Society: The Afikpo Village-Group. Seattle: University of Washington Press.

Penfield, Joyce. 1981. "Quoting Behavior in Igbo Society." Research in African Literatures, 12, 3: 309-337.

Peters, H. 1971. "Reflections on the Preservation of Igbo Folk Literature," The Conch, 3, 2: 97-103.

Prince, R. 1960. "Curse, Invocation and Mental Health Among the Yoruba," Canadian Psychiatric Association Journal, 5, 2: 65-79.

Quinn, N. 1976. "A Natural System Used in Mfantse Litigation Settlement," American Ethnologist, 3: 331-351.

Radcliffe-Brown, A. R. 1935. "On the Concept of Function in Social Science," American Anthropologist, 37: 394-395.

_____, ed., 1950. African Systems of Kinship and Marriage. New York: Oxford University Press.

Bibliography

Radcliffe-Brown, A. R. 1952. <u>Structure and Function in Primitive Society</u>. London: Cohen and West.

Redfield, R. 1952. "The Primitive World View," <u>Proceedings of the American Philosophical Society</u>, 96: 30-36.

_____. 1953. <u>The Primitive World and Its Transformations</u>. Ithaca, New York: Cornell University Press.

_____. 1956. <u>The Little Community</u>. Chicago: The University of Chicago Press.

Sacks, H. 1972. "On Some Puns with some Intimations," in R. Shuy, ed., <u>Sociolinguistics: Current Trends and Prospects</u>. Georgetown University Monograph Series on Languages and Linguistics 25: Washington, D.C.

_____. 1974. "An Analysis of the Course of a Joke's Telling in Conversation," in R. Bauman and J. Sherzer, eds., <u>Explorations in the Ethnography of Speaking</u>. New York: Cambridge University Press, 337-353.

Schegloff, E. and Sacks, H. 1969. "Opening up Closings," Expanded version of a paper presented at the annual meetings of the American Sociological Association, San Francisco, Sept. 1969.

Searle, J. 1973. "What is a Speech Act?" in P. Giglioli, ed., <u>Language and Social Context</u>. Baltimore, Md.: Penguin Books, 136-154.

Seitel, Peter. 1969. "Proverbs: A Social Use of Metaphor," <u>Genre</u> 2: 143-161.

_____. 1972. "Proverbs and the Structure of Metaphor Among the Haya of Tanzania," Ph.D. dissertation. University of Pennsylvania.

Shelton, A. J. 1969. "The 'Palm-Oil' of Language: Proverbs in Chinua Achebe's Novels," <u>Modern Language Quarterly</u>, 30: 86-111.

_____. 1971. "Relativism, Pragmatism, and Reciprocity in Igbo Proverbs," <u>The Conch</u>, 3, 2: 46-62.

Sherzer, J. 1977. "The Ethnography of Speaking: A Critical Appraisal," Paper presented at the 28th Annual Georgetown University Round Table on Languages and Linguistics, Washington, D.C., March 1977.

Society for Promoting Igbo Language and Culture (*Otu Iwelite Asusu Na Omenala Igbo*). n.d. <u>Recommendation of the Standardization Committee</u>, Vol. I, Onitsha, Nigeria: Varsity Industrial Press, Limited.

Southall, A. 1959. "An Operational Theory of Role," <u>Human Relations</u>, 12: 17-34.

Stross, B. 1974. "Speaking of Speaking: Tenejapa Tzeltal Metalinguistics," in R. Bauman and J. Sherzer, eds., <u>Explorations in the Ethnography of Speaking</u>. New York: Cambridge University Press, 213-239.

Tambiah, S. J. 1968. "The Magical Power of Words," <u>Man</u>, 3.2: 175-208.

Uchendu, V. 1965. <u>The Igbo of Southeast Nigeria</u>. New York: Holt, Rinehart, and Winston.

Welmers, B. F. and Welmers, Wm. E. 1968. <u>Igbo: A Learner's Dictionary</u>. Los Angeles, California: African Studies Center.

Welmers, Wm. E. 1973. <u>African Language Structures</u>. Berkeley: University of California Press.

Westermarck, E. A. 1930. <u>Wit and Wisdom in Morocco: A Study of Native Proverbs</u>. London: Routledge.

Winner, Thomas G. 1979. "Jan Mukařovský: The Beginnings of Structural Semiotic Aesthetics," in <u>Language, Literature and Meaning I: Problems of Literary Theory</u>, edited by John Odmark. <u>Linguistic and Literary Studies in Eastern Europe</u>, Vol. I. Amsterdam: John Benjamins, B.V., pp. 1-34.

Wölck, W. 1975. "Report on Scoiolinguistic Survey Planning in the Andean Republics," Paper presented at the International Conference on Methodology of Sociolinguistic Surveys, Montreal, Quebec, May 19, 1975.

──────. 1976. "Community Profiles: An Alternative Approach to Linguistic Informant Selection," eds., J. P. Rona and W. Wolck in <u>The Social Dimension of Dialectology</u> (IJSL, 9) The Hague: Mouton, 43-57.

Zamora, M., J. M. Mahar, and H. Orenstein, eds., 1971. <u>Themes in Culture (Essays in Honor of Morris E. Opler)</u>, Quezon City, Philippines: Kayumanggi Publishers.

GENERAL SUBJECT INDEX

Abel, R.L., 73-74

Abomination (arū̇), 36,73

Abrahams, R.D., 2

Accused. See Interactional roles

Adversary. See Interactional roles

Advise (ídū̇ odū̇), 50-52,55,58, 62-64,94,106-7

Advisee. See Interactional roles

Advisor. See Interactional roles

Afikpo, 78

Àmàmíhe. See Intelligence

Ancestors, 9,19-20,22,32,35, 37-39,42,45,47

Archaic lexicon, 6

Arewa, E.O., 2,62,88

Authoritativeness. See Ancestors; Proverbs, functional properties of

Azande. See Proverbs, Africa

Backbite (ímebí áhā̇ mmadù̇), 50-53,60-67,109. See also Conflict, stages of

Bascom, W.R., 84

Benedict, Ruth, 83

Bergsma, H.M., 88

Biblical sayings. See Quotes, types of

Bilinguals, Igbo-English, 2,4, 24-25,85-87

Bird, C., 90

Bühler, Karl, 22

Cartoons, 79

Character. See Reputation

Christensen, J.B., 2

Christian community, 4

Christianity, 1,86

Collective conscience, Igbo, 81. See also Cultural themes

Conflict (èsèmokwu): covert, 58-61; folk conception of, 47-48,74,93; offenses leading to, 49-50; overt, 60; stages of development, 28, 33,48-61,106-10; theory of, 28,73-74; use of quotes, 1, 4,47-54. See also Interactional roles; Interpersonal roles; Mediation; Speech events

"Context," 6,17-19. See also Bühler; Interactional setting; Mukařovský

Court settlement (íkpē̇ íkpe), 48,52-54,110. See also Conflict, stages of

Craftiness. See Cultural themes; Intelligence

Cultural themes, 20-21; definition of, 76-77,83; Igbo, 76-84. See also Indirectness; Intelligence; Skill

Culture, 20-21. See also Cultural themes, Igbo

General Subject Index   135

"Deautomization," 6,16. *See also* Mukařovský

Depersonalization. *See* Indirectness, verbal; Proverbs, functional properties of

"Desubjectivization," 19-20,98. *See also* Mukařovský

Dialects, Igbo. *See* Onitsha, dialect; Owerri, dialect

Disputant. *See* Interactional roles

Dundes, Alan, 3,62,88

Emenanjọ, E.N., 15,23

"Enemy." *See* Interpersonal roles

English literature. *See* Quotes, types of

English sayings. *See* Quotes, types of

Èsèmokwu. *See* Conflict

Ethnography of communication, 1,14,20-22,76-77; field methods, 24-27; fundamental assumptions, 20-24; proverbs, 88-90; quoting behavior, 3, 31-75. *See also* Conflict; Indirectness, verbal; Interactional roles; Proverbs, Africa; Proverbs, usage; Quoting Behavior; Skill

Evans-Pritchard, E.E., 33,90

"Exchange of words" (*iliā olilia*). *See* Conflict, stages of; Verbal duel

Fante. *See* Proverbs, Africa

Finnegan, Ruth, 1,4,88,90

Folk conception, 2-3,23-24,44-46

Folk explanation, 24,29

Folktale, 76-77

Folk term, 24,29

Folk verbal account, 2-3,15,24; examples of, 5-7,11,54-57, 59-68

Forde, C.D., 32,73

Foregrounding. *See* "Context;" Proverbs, functional properties of

"Friend." *See* Interpersonal roles

Functional properties. *See* Proverbs, functional properties of

Functions of language: immediate, 3,15,68; theory, 2,15, 20; ultimate, 3,15. *See also* Bühler; Garvin; Hymes; Language, external function; Language, functionalist view; Mathiot; Mukařovský; Proverbs, functional properties of

Garvin, Paul, 15,20,22-23,75, 96-104

Gladwin, C., 75

Green, Margaret, 74

Greenhouse, Carol, 4,88

Guided recall, 24-25,29. *See also* Folk verbal account

Gumperz, John, 14

Herskovits, M.J., 2

Hymes, Dell, 1-2,49

Ibibio, Anang. *See* Proverbs, Africa

Ibo. See Igbo language; Igbo society

Igbo language, 29-30; orthography, 13-14; sounds, 13-14; tones, 13-14,16. See also Onitsha Igbo, dialect; Owerri Igbo, dialect

Igbo society, 1,4,27; demography, 31-32; ethnography of, 72; language, 29

Imo state, 2,32

Indirectness, verbal, 3,66,86; appreciation of, 11-12; politeness, 11; skill, 77-78. See also Cartoons; Depersonalization; Folktales; Intelligence; Meaning; Nwoga; Proverbs, Africa; Proverbs, internal aspects; Proverbs, usage; Quoting behavior; Skill; Song and dance; "Speaking in general statements"; "Using words carelessly"

In-laws. See Social groups, in-laws

Insult (*mkpari*), 7,11,50-52,55, 106. See also Conflict, stages of

Intelligence, 7,11-12,40-46,62-71,80-81. See also Skill

Interactional event. See Speech event

Interactional roles, 35,44-46, 71; adversary, 51,59-61,66-67; advisor-advisee, 51,54-55, 62-64; mediator-disputant, 5, 38,57-68; offended-accused, 43-44,51,57-58,64-66

Interactional setting, 2-19,24-25,28

Interpersonal roles, 35,44-46; "enemy", 5-6,43-44; "friend", 43

Intimidate (*imenye egwū*), 50-52, 55-56,61,107. See also Conflict, stages of

Jones, G.I., 32,73

Kinship, 42. See also Social groups, kinbased

Kluckhohn, C., 21,83

Language: assumptions about, 20-24; external function, 23-24; field-derived characteristics 22-23; functionalist view, 4, 15,20; systerm-derived characteristics, 22-23. See also Functions of language

"Law of the land" (*omenàlà*), 12, 36-39,42,44-48,56,72

Leadership, 42,70-71

Maninka. See Proverbs, Africa

Mathiot, Madeleine, 15,20,22. See also Language, functionalist view

Meaning, of proverbs: literal, 10,14; philosophical, 10,14

Mediation (*idozī okwu*), 40-41, 45,50,57-58,67-68,75,108,110. See also Conflict, stages of

Mediator. See Interactional roles

Messenger, J.C., 88

Metaphor. See Proverbs, internal aspects

Mukařovský, Jan, 2-3,6,8,14,16-20,87,96-104

Norms and values, reference to. See Proverbs, functional properties of

Nwoga, D.I., 16,19,23,78

General Subject Index   137

Offended. *See* Interactional roles

Offenses, 36,49,74. *See also* Conflict, offenses leading to; Law of the land; Taboo

Ọ̀fọ, 72. *See also* Law of the land

Ogbalu, F.C., 22

Okigwe township, 25,27

Olisa, M.S.O., 81

Omenàlà. *See* Law of the land

Onitsha Igbo, 29; dialect, 30

Onitsha Province, 29-30

Onwu Orthography, 13-14,25

Opler, M., 20,83

"Ordinary" language, 2-3,14-15, 70

Ottenberg, S., 32,70-72,75,78

Owerri Igbo, 2-3,29,31-50,72; dialect, 25,29-30; social units, 33-35

Owerri Province, 25,30-31

Owerri township, 25,27,29,31

Patrilineage (ụmụ̀ nnà). *See* Social groups, kin based

Persuasion. *See* Skill

Peters, H., 78

Pidgin English, 85

Prague school. *See* Bühler, Garvin, Mukařovský

Prestige. *See* Proverbs, functional properties of; Skill, quoting

Prevention, 79-81. *See also* Cultural themes

Proverbs, Africa, 1-2,17-19,88; Anang Ibibio, 88; Azande, 90; Fante, 2; Igbo, 1-2,5,7-8, 10-11,44,54-68,77-78,86,111-20; Maninka, 90; Tiv, 88

Proverbs, America: Arkansas, 89; Georgia, 88

Proverbs, Europe, 8,20

Proverbs, functional properties of: authoritativeness, 5,8-9; depersonalization, 5-6,11,19, 66-68,88-89; foregrounding, 5-8,16; prestige, 5,10-12,68; norms and values, reference to, 10

Proverbs, internal aspects: introducers, 22; lexicon, 6,9, 15,19; linguistic devices, 6,15-16,22-23; linguistic structure, 6-7,15-16,19,23; metaphor, 7; nature of, 3-4, 22-23; poetic devices, 23; semantic reference, 6,9-10, 18,20

Proverbs, usage: "corrective", 19; "illuminative", 19; judicial, 88-90. *See also* Finnegan; Proverbs, America; Proverbs, Europe; Quoting behavior

Quotes, types of: Biblical sayings, English literature, English sayings, 1,4,8,10,22, 85-87; Igbo proverbs, 1-2,5, 7-8,10-11,44,54-68,77-78,86, 111-120. *See also* Conflict; Indirectness, verbal; Interactional roles; Mukařovský; Proverbs, Africa; Proverbs, functional properties of; Proverbs, internal aspects of; Proverbs, usage; Quoting behavior; Skill

General Subject Index

Quoting behavior: definition of, 1; ethnography of, 1-3; folk conception of, 3-4; function of, in Igbo society, 1,3,23-24; researching, 2-3,14,24-27; theory of, 2,6,14,17-20; univerals of, 4,90-91; worldwide, 87-91. See also Conflict; Herskovits; Indirectness, verbal; Interactional roles; Mukařovský; Proverbs, Africa; Proverbs, functional properties of; Proverbs, internal aspects; Proverbs, usage; Quotes, types of; Skill

Redfield, A.R., 20

Reincarnation, 38

Reputation, 9,36,44,59,66,81-82

Rhetoric, tools of. See Indirectness, verbal

Roles. See Interactional roles; Interpersonal roles; Social roles

Sacred. See Ancestors; ọ́sọ; Law of the land

Scott, R., 32

Shopen, T., 90

Situation. See Interactional setting; Speech event

Skill: quoting, 4,7-12,24,44, 46,55,62-71,77,80-81; role enactment, 68-71,77-79. See also Indirectness,verbal; Intelligence

Slander. See Backbite

Social groups: in-laws, 35,39-40; kin based, 32-29,48-50, 72; non-kin based, 34,40-42, 48-50

Social roles, 33-35,44-46,73, 75; kin based, 35-40;

Social roles (continued) non-kin based, 40-42. See also Ancestors; Law of the land

Song and dance, 16,42,78

"Speaking in general statements" (ikpē ìkpè), 16,50-53, 59,77,83

Speech event, 50-54. See also Advise; Backbite; Conflict, stages of development; Court case; Insult; Intimidate; Mediation; Verbal duel

Status position, 24,33,35,36, 70-71,82

Taboo (nsọ), 36

"Theatricalization," 18. See also Mukařovský

Theme. See Cultural themes

"Third-party intrusion," 16-18. See Mukařovský

Tiv. See Proverbs, Africa

Tradition. See Ancestors; Prestige

Uchendu, Victor, 38,42,47,74, 79,81

"Using words carelessly" (ìmé akàjà), 16,77,83

Uturu community, 25,27,42

Verbal duel (ìlìā olìlìa), 50-53,57-58,66-67,74,107. See also Conflict, stages of development

Welmers, W., 14

Worldview. See Cultural themes

Zamora, M., 76

About the Author

JOYCE PENFIELD received her Ph.D. in linguistics from the State University of New York at Buffalo. She is currently an Assistant Professor of Language Education in the Graduate School of Education at Rutgers University, New Brunswick, New Jersey. She has written *Chicano English—An Ethnic Border Dialect* (with J. Ornstein), and articles in *Bilingual Education Paper Series, Handbook on Black Communication, Research in African Literature, Anthropological Linguistics,* and *Kiábara.*

OHIO UNIVERSITY LIBRARY

Please return this book as soon as you have finished with it. In order to avoid a fine it must be returned by the latest date stamped below. All books are subject to recall after two weeks or immediately if needed for reserve.

CF